Practical Crystal Healing

Practical Crystal Healing

*555 Tips & Techniques
For Animal Companions*

Nicole Lanning

© 2010 Nicole Lanning

All rights reserved. No part of this book may be reproduced, stored in a retrieval system, or transmitted by any means without written permission of the author.

First published 8/2010
ISBN: 1453750339

Printed in the United States of America

To my soul mate and husband, Jonathon, our two inspiring children, Reiss and Phebe, and all of our animal companions Bugzee, Brinkley, Sophie, Inky, and Mocha.

Healing Love

To have their love in your life is a magical blessing. Then one day you hear the news that you never wanted to hear. What do you do now? Where do you turn? How can you help?

They were there for you every step of the way. Every time you were down and out. Every time you were jumping for joy. It didn't matter to them, because all they knew was love for you.

The vet says something is wrong and you don't know what to do. Look into their eyes and feel the love. They know what to do. There is only love in their heart and soul.

Try what you can, and from every avenue, to help and heal their issues, hurt, and pain. They were there for you, now it is your turn to be there for them. You are all they have!

They will not be disappointed and they will not hold any grudges. They love you with all of their hearts. As long as you try, that is all that they ask of you. That, and to be by their side every step of the way!

- Nicole Lanning

CONTENTS

Chapter 1.	Crystal Healing For Animals Introduction	1
Chapter 2.	Crystal Healing Basics For Animals	5
Chapter 3.	Crystal Usage	 13
Chapter 4.	Animal Healing Basics	17
Chapter 5.	Animal Signs	21
Chapter 6.	Animal Chakra Centers	27
Chapter 7.	Animal Aura Levels	33
Chapter 8.	Crystal Pendulum Dowsing	37
Chapter 9.	Crystal Healing Kits For Animals	41
Chapter 10.	555 Crystal Healing Tips & Techniques	45

x

Introduction

Animals, of all sorts, have a special place in our hearts. They come in all shapes and sizes from dogs and cats to horses, birds, fish, and reptiles. Once they enter our lives, hearts, and souls an exceptional place is created that no one can ever fill again. We can, however, expand and open ourselves for more animals to enter throughout our own lifetime. They allow us to share our unconditional love in such a unique way that only our true heart and soul can understand.

There are so many animals out in the world today that they need our help just as much as we seek their unconditional love in our lives. So many we come across are abandoned, abused, neglected, hurt, or even dying. We open ourselves to these wonderful creatures in every way possible to give them a fighting chance at a wonderful and happy life. Unfortunately, some of them have already dealt with many issues in their lives that they have emotional scaring along with physical ailments. This is where we come in and start to heal from the very core to help these animals become a permanent part of our lives.

This book was an instant stepping-stone from my previous book, Practical Crystal Healing: 555 Tips & Techniques. After writing this book, I received many emails and phone calls asking if the techniques could be used for animals. It made sense that if I wrote a book for human crystal healing, our animal counterparts needed a book too. They deal with some of the issues we face in our human existence, but are often misunderstood with the communication gap.

This topic has hit home on so many occasions in my own personal life as well, with currently having four canines of our own, they run into physical problems and health concerns just as much as humans can. We had our own little bout with our dearly departed little one, Bugzee, as he was only in our lives until he was three months old before we had to send his spirit to the other side. Bugzee was a fighter all the way, and helped me experience a part of myself through healing of animals that I had to learn in order to write this book.

There are 555 tips and techniques in this book that cover physical issues, mental issues, emotional concerns, and even spiritual topics, and all working with your animal companions. Prior to diving into these tips, each chapter gives you a bit on different aspects of animal healing and how to approach them, basic healing concerns, and even crystal kits to have on hand. It really is a beginner through advanced book for anyone who loves his or her animal companions, complimentary therapies, and has a willingness to help and learn!

All of the tips and techniques in this book can be used on our pets, offered as healing for other animals, and can even be used on wildlife animals that we may encounter in our backyard, local park, or forest. Remember key points in working with animals is letting go, trusting, following your intuition, mutual respect that is shared and incorporating an energetic connection with the healing that you provide through the use of crystals. Listen to the animal companions first with an open heart and centered mind and you will always be able to provide them with attention, love, affection, and validation.

Disclaimer: The information given in this book is not intended to act as a substitute for medical treatment or advice from a physician, medical provider, or veterinarian, nor can it be used to diagnosis any ailment, issue, or disease. Make sure you use crystal healing as a complimentary service in conjunction with your veterinarian's guidelines.

Chapter 1:
Crystal Healing For Animals Introduction

Crystals are powerful "living rocks" and can often be misunderstood.

Crystal healing is a wonderful addition to alternative types of health and well-being programs, especially for our animal companions. Let me start off by saying that crystal healing, at its basic level, is about balancing the energy of a person, animal, or environment back to a harmonious state within the physical body or area to ease the problem, issue, or imbalance at hand. You can start today in working with crystal healing for humans and animals.

Our pets and animals have ailments, problems, and issues just as much as we do. They develop physical, mental, emotional, and even spiritual issues that need help. Some of these issues can be seen such as behavior problems or even major physical ailments such as sores or fur falling out, but there are many underlying issues that animals have to deal with too.

Animals experience stress and trauma, but cannot communicate this to us through verbal words.

I have researched both extremes on this matter when working with my own animal companions. Some scientists believe that animals cannot really think or reason, as they believe that all of their behaviors are done without planning, insight, or even thought. This would mean our animal companions are nothing more than mere robots. If you have ever had an animal companion in your lifetime, have spent time with this loved one, and truly allowed your heart and soul to love unconditionally, I believe that 99% of us would say that our animal companions are more than mere robots.

There is also the other end of the spectrum that says animals are capable of reasoning and mental process, just as people are. This goes to say that the mental network is of a simple nature compared to human mental reasoning. We, as humans, have intricate thought patterns, similar to having a mini computer in our physical heads. Animals have this same computer, but on a smaller scale. Our mental wiring is capable of infinite possibilities, with many of them not even being understood still today. Animal's mental wiring is less intricate, complex, and more emotional based within their energetic fields. My personal opinion, with the work I have seen and done, I favor this explanation. I believe that animals do have a mental process, feelings, emotions, and so much more. They are just on a simpler scale than what we perceive in our own conscious reality.

If they experience this reasoning capability, than one could wonder if animals can communicate with us about the issues that are going on within their own physical beings. With research, study, meditation, and my own guided work I believe that animals do communicate, just in a different way than we were brought up to understand.

You have probably seen the Dr. Dolittle movies that show an animal and the doctor or family member communicating with the animals as they would a human. Animals do this to a certain extent, but we do not hear them (for the most part) with our physical ears as we do our human counter-parts. Just because we do not hear them in such a way does not mean we are not communicating with them or they with us. This is just a language barrier. They are normally "heard", depending on the person they are interacting with, on a mental and emotional level, through communication. Our animal companions love crystal energies just as much as we do but with this communication gap, it can be overlooked and misunderstood on how to use them.

Animals, in fact, have a very high vibrational level output and can handle a large amount of energy. This has nothing to do with their shape or size, but rather this has to deal with their energetic fields and the innocence, understanding, and unconditional love energy that surround their very physical forms. They actually process healing energy very quickly and effortlessly and much easier than humans can. Their aura levels and chakra centers absorb this so quickly that the healing sessions do not take as long as human energy levels or even an environmental energy grid can for a healing session.

Working with animals requires practice, patience, and persistence; the three P's. With practice, in an animal healing session, you will learn overtime the key signs that animals have had enough energy and to end the session. You will also learn when the animal wants more energy, for the crystal to be placed in a different area, or just a general thank you from the animal for the work you are providing for them. Patience will come through this type of work too. With this communication gap in place, animals are not always the most patient and can be hard to handle, but with your practice and patience combined, you can make the healing session even more successful. Add persistence to this mix and the animal crystal healing session will be victorious.

A winning combination of the healing energies, your desire to help the animal in need, and the animal's desire to want to be healed; along with your practice, patience, and persistence, you can start on a wonderful new pathway through your own life in helping our animal companions.

Chapter 2:
Crystal Healing Basics For Animals

Crystal healing basics are the same whether they are used for humans or animals. The same process is applied whether they are for cleansing, programming, or charging them.

You can cleanse your crystals in a variety of ways. The top suggested cleansing methods involve a type of energetic vibrational cleansing generally coming from nature elements. Cleansing your crystals is a very important process because you want to make sure that they are at the highest healing level possible when performing your work. Cleansing provides this for your crystals. If you are someone who only uses your crystals occasionally and simply place them back in the healing bag, you are carrying around a lot of unnecessary energetic debris. The debris is from the healing session that the crystal was used for, and if not properly cleansed, can still be attached to the crystal's energy fields when working on any future healings. There are a few crystals out there that do not hold onto the energetic imprints, so for these crystals it is not required to cleanse them as often, but they can still be cleansed and programmed regularly to give their vibrational rate a much needed energetic boost. You want to show your crystals that you care and respect the vibrational energy that they share with us for healing purposes, and a good way to do this is by cleansing them!

Programming is a way of telling your crystals what you wish them to do for a particular healing session. This is especially helpful when working with animals, as you will need to have them programmed ahead of time so that they are aware of your intention with the work you want to accomplish. This will increase the vibrational output from the crystal, as they will know what you are working on for a particular animal. If you do not have time to pre-program your crystals, please do not worry though as they will still provide a generous output of vibrational healing.

When you program your crystals for specific purposes in your healing sessions they have a direct connection with you and know what you want them to do. If you are working on an animal that has an aggressive behavioral issue, and you program the crystal for this reason it is immediately going to start working on the aggression issue first and secondly send out any extra healing that is needed, and in this order. When you do not program them for a specific reason in your healing session, maybe because you don't know what the animal is dealing with on an energy level or maybe you just didn't have time to program your crystal before your session begins, please do not be concerned. The crystal healing session will still be effective. What will happen is a reverse response on how the vibrational energy is sent. Let's use the example of an aggression issue with the animal you are working on, but you didn't have time to program your crystal. What will happen is the energy will first provide a general energy from the crystal for the animal and if the animal is still allowing the acceptance of the energy, then it will start to tackle the aggression issue. Either way the animal is receiving the healing energy from the crystal, but a programmed crystal will provide a stronger healing session at first as this will tackle the problem head on, not secondary.

Charging your crystals is a way of programming them, but incorporates the use of energy in with your work. You can charge a crystal with a form of Reiki, solar, lunar, water, or Mother Earth energy. Charging is a way of saying it is programmed for what you want including an extra energetic vibrational frequency. This can come from all sorts of places, so let your mind be open and expand and see where you can draw on more energy sources available to you.

CLEANSING YOUR CRYSTALS

Smudging, water cleansing, solar energy, sound vibrations, and many other techniques are used for cleansing. Pick what resonates best for you for that particular crystal and the healing session that was provided. Some crystals work better when they are cleansed with smudging, while others work better with a water cleanse. Practice and experiment with different forms to provide the best possible cleansing sessions for your crystals and animal companions.

Sage smudge cleansing can be done by simply passing your crystal back and forth through the smudge smoke 4 times in each direction, so a total of 8 times. I prefer to turn the crystal after each pass. When you do pass the crystal through the smoke it will push through each session and the smoke will pass over, under, and around the crystal. By turning this though, you will make sure to increase the effectiveness for the entire physical part of the crystal and the energetic fields that are surrounding it.

Water cleansing is a quick and effective way to cleanse your crystals too. For harder stones, you can place them in a glass bowl of purified water with a small amount of sea salt and let them soak for 1 hour. For softer stones, you can simply hold them in your hand as you thoroughly drench them with a room temperature bottle of purified water.

Sea salt mounds a good way to cleanse your crystals with this absorbing type of energy without the damaging effects that water and sea salt can have on the softer stones. For a sea salt mound, make sure you pour an appropriate amount of coarse sea salt onto a glass plate to begin. Next, place your crystals on this salt mound and allow them to rest overnight. The sea salt will absorb the crystals energetic debris and imprints to bring their vibrational level back to an effervescent healing state. This type of cleansing is a good one to use even for the crystals that do not need to be cleansed, as this gives them a break from the healing sessions and allows them to recharge quickly.

Solar energy is an excellent way to cleanse your crystals, but please do note that the sun's rays can fade some of the crystal's coloration. To use this type of cleansing and charging, you can use your water cleanse as instructed above for the softer crystals, and then simply place your crystal in the sunlight to dry and charge. I would recommend putting them somewhere you can watch them, as they do not take long to dry, and this way you can prevent them from to much exposure to the heat and fading of colors.

Lunar energy cleansing is an exciting way to incorporate the moon's energy with a cleansing session. The only recommendation I make for this type of cleansing is to either place them in a secure location outside, where they will not be disturbed by curious wildlife, or to keep them inside on a window ledge so they can absorb the lunar energy but are still safe. Full moon energies are the best for cleansing, but crystals can be cleansed all through the lunar cycle if so chosen.

Rain cleansing is an interesting way to combine a water cleansing session and a natural Earth element. Simply place your crystals outside during a gentle rain shower for at least 30 minutes. Rain cleansing is much quicker than typical water cleansing because this incorporates the Earth energy into the cleansing process. Remember to gently dry the crystals after each cleanse.

Sound vibrational cleansing is a pleasurable way to cleanse your crystals. You can use different instruments to provide this type of work, such as a tuning fork, bell, drum, Tibetan singing bowl, and Tibetan cymbals to name just a few. For sound vibration cleansing, you would use the appropriate method to activate the sound and place your crystals as close to this as possible. When using a tuning fork, bell, or drums, you can place them next to the vibration. For the Tibetan singing bowl you would hold your crystals within the inside interior of the bowl while the sound continues. When using your Tibetan cymbals, you will strike them together and then place the crystal in-between the cymbals for the sound cleansing to occur.

There are also a few other ways for cleansing your crystals, such as Mother Earth, fire, sand, mirror, and sage tea cleansing. Mother Earth energy cleansing is a simple process of burying your crystal, surrounded in cheesecloth and silk, for 24 hours. Fire energy is a long and time old tradition, but can damage your crystals, so please be careful with this one. You can pass your crystal through the fire flame three times for this to be cleansed. Sand cleansing can be done by burying your crystal in moist sand for two hours and rinsing thoroughly afterwards. Make note that sand cleansing can damage the polish off tumbled stones and can scratch natural crystals too. For mirror cleansing, simply place your crystal on top of a mirror facing upward and leave there overnight. The mirror will reflect back and outward any issues needed to be cleansed off the crystal. Sage tea cleansing is a wonderful combination of water and sage to use effectively for your crystals. Brew a pot of sage infused tea and let cool. Pour the sage tea over your crystals in a glass bowl and allow them to bathe overnight. In the morning, rinse them with purified water and dry. All of these techniques are wonderful in their own right, but remember to use what resonates within you and your crystal work for the cleansing session.

PROGRAMMING & CHARGING YOUR CRYSTALS

Programming is performed within one of two ways, a Passive or an Active Method. These are both very simple and easy to use. Remember to always follow your intuition and go with what resonates within you while programming or charging your crystals.

The Passive Method is the easiest of all, and can be done by anyone. This simply states that you use the same crystal repeatedly for the same ailment. So let's use the aggression issue we talked about earlier in this book, as you would use a Blue Lace Agate for this type of problem. You could simply use the same Blue Lace Agate over and over for each aggression session you performed, with cleansing in-between. The one reason I do not prefer this method is due to the timing factor involved. Let's say you only have one crystal healing session for this issue and do not have another one for 2 weeks, or even two months. Your Blue Lace Agate, if used in the meantime for other ailments, will not understand what its main purpose is for that particular healing at any given time. This is the easiest way to program a crystal and if used for the same purpose repeatedly within a short amount of time, the crystal will accept the programming quickly and easily.

The Active Method takes a bit more concentration and intention to program, but is still very easy to do, even for the beginners out there. For this method, you can simply place the appropriate crystal in your hand, close your eyes and project on an energetic level to the crystal what you wish its sole purpose to be at this time. With the aggression issue we talked about, you would hold the Blue Lace Agate in your dominant hand, close your eyes and simply use your connection with the crystal to ask that it be used for aggression issues at this time for this particular session. Use your intention with this method and that's all that it takes!

For the active method to work through, you will need to make sure you have the appropriate crystal for the session. Let's take the Blue Lace Agate again, and this crystal is wonderful for working with aggression, clawing, inflammation, walking, and many other uses for our animal companions. You would not, however, use this crystal for working on something such as ear problems, eating problems, fear of noises, or lice issues, as Amber works well for these. When trying to program a crystal for something that is not within its vibrational level match, the programming will not "stick" or "hold." You can try to program it for issues that are not within its vibrational match, but as soon as you let go of your **intention** within your mind the programming will let go of the crystal and fall to the side. So please make sure you are using the appropriate crystals and programming when performing this work.

Charging your crystals provides an extra boost to healing sessions. A Reiki charge can not only heal any issues the crystal has, but also incorporates the Universal Source energy called Reiki and holds this within its vibrational fields. You must be at least a Usui

Reiki Level 1 to be able to charge your crystals for healing work. With my extensive work with channeling energy forms, when you use the appropriate energy combined with the crystal healing this creates a powerful healing session. For working with animals, I would recommend using an animal based energy form for charging sessions. This not only creates a stronger vibrational output for the crystal, but this also allows an energized connection between you, your crystal, and the animal companion you are working with at that time. The animal will benefit from both the crystal energy and the charge that you have established through the crystal.

To charge a crystal for a healing session, hold the crystal in between the palms of your hands. Holding it at your palm chakra creates a potent connection for the energy flow. Next, start your Reiki energy flow out your palm chakras and surrounding the crystal. You want to make sure you are using the energy form that you have activated, not your own personal energy, and are pulling from the Universal Source. Ask that the crystal be healed and now have access to the energy form that you are using, whether it is Usui Reiki or another energy form. Keep running the energy through your palm chakras until the energy pull from the crystal has disconnected on its own.

Solar, lunar, rain, and Mother Earth energy can charge crystals in a very simple fashion. Place the crystal in its appropriate place (such as under the Full Moon or in a spring rain shower) and allow the crystal to absorb the charge from the nature elements. Nature elements bring a natural energy boost to all crystals during the charge. You want to make sure you use an appropriate crystal for the specific nature element you want to charge with, as certain crystals can rust if exposed to rain and others can fade with solar energy. Remember to take care of your crystals and their energies, and they will in turn help take care of you!

Chapter 3:
Crystal Usage

Crystal healing for animals is actually very easy to do once you start working with them. I have broken the tips and techniques into easy to understand forms of how to use them for each individual use. All of the tips and techniques described in this book are intended to work for the majority of animals, comprising of dogs, cats, horses, birds, fish, reptiles, wildlife, and any other kids of animal companion in your life. The majority of these tips and techniques are comprised of one of three areas: Wearing, Grid Placement, or Elixirs/Mists. Each one is a bit different, so please read the entire technique before trying this on your animal companion.

Wearing a crystal is very effective and an easy way to help the animals in your life. When searching for pendants for your animals to wear make sure they can secure easily and stay fastened tightly before attaching them to a collar or harness permanently. When attaching the crystal(s) make sure they are not hanging to low where the animal can chew or possibly swallow them. You should always make sure the crystal is snug inside its casing, wire wrap, or enclosure.

You can also attach crystals using a small type of medicine bag and attaching this to the animal's collar or harness. This is a particularly good idea when using multiple crystals for different reasons. Remember to cleanse and program the crystals for the appropriate reason before placing them in the bag. You want to start with only one or two crystals in the medicine bag. If you place too many crystals in a medicine bag at once, when the animal is not used to the crystal energy, it can be a bit overwhelming for them and difficult to integrate all of the healing vibration at once. They may become disoriented until their energetic fields are aligned with the healing that is being sent through the crystals. It is best to start with one or two and add more later on when they are adjusted to the new healing. Be careful that the pouch does not interfere with movement in anyway, as you do not want them to start chewing at this for comfort reasons.

Grid placement simply means you are placing the crystals around in a certain area or position for the most effective energy usage. This can refer to the animal's crate, cage, bedding, stable, aquarium, or even the general place that the animal spends his/her time, such as in a particular part of your home. There are intricate grid systems that you can work with for crystal healing, but when working with animals, simple works best for all concerned. This eliminates the time in setting up the grids and allows you to focus on the animal and the healing that needs to transpire. Again, make sure these are not within chewing capabilities or cannot be swallowed by the animal.

Elixirs and mists are a wonderful way to combine not only the energy healing of water but also the crystal's vibrational energy to help heal the issues that are being addressed. You can make elixirs and mists with a purified water base, the appropriate crystal, and a glass bottle for storage. Because there are so many different crystals available to use for healing and some include harmful toxins if ingested, it is recommended either an indirect crystal charge or a crystal within a charge are made for these types of crystal elixirs and mists. If you wish to use a direct crystal charge elixir, make sure that the crystals do not contain any form of copper, lead, zinc, sulphur, mercury, aluminum, or any other harmful toxins.

A Direct Charge is a very simple process to complete. Place a glass bowl on the counter and your crystal inside the bowl. Next pour purified bottled water over the crystal. Let the crystal charge the water for the minimum time required for each technique. Remove the crystal and pour the charged water into your glass bottle. Make sure to have everything as clean as possible, from the crystal to the bowl and the glass bottle you are using for storage. This charge is recommended for crystals that do not include harmful toxins.

An Indirect Crystal Charge is when you place purified water in a glass bowl and place the crystal on the outside of the bowl. The water will absorb the crystal's energies without even touching the crystal, so there is no need to worry about direct contact. The water needs to charge for the appropriate amount of time for each specific issue. After the allotted amount of time for the crystal charge, pour the water into your storage bottle. This is a recommended use for crystals that contain harmful toxins.

A Crystal Within a Charge is a bit more complicated, but has a wonderful energy output when used for elixirs and mists. For this type of charge, you will need two glass bowls, one smaller than the first. Place your larger glass bowl on the counter, and then place the smaller one inside of the larger one. Next, pour the purified water in the larger bowl so that it surrounds the smaller bowl. Last, place your crystal in the smaller bowl and allow the water to charge. After the water is finished charging, remove the crystal first, then the smaller bowl, and finally pour the charged water into your glass bottle. Your crystal is the last thing in and the first thing out, so there is no direct contact with the water. You want to do these steps in this order, as this will make sure that if water is splashed it will not touch the crystal in anyway.

Chapter 4:
Animal Healing Basics

Healing animals is not much different than working with our human energy fields, but there does seem to be confusion when it comes to crystal healing and animals in general. The confusion lies within the lack of education about this topic, as well as the communication factor in working with animals. These precious little companions are like you and me. They each have their own brain, heart, lungs, legs, and skin and are living breathing creatures. Just because they may not speak our language doesn't mean they aren't dealing with ailments, behavioral issues, physical diseases, and ordinary things such as allergies, colds, aches, and pains. So why is it so hard for a lot of people to learn how to treat them on a physical level?

Crystal healing requires a very strong and centered mind, body, and spirit connection. I cannot stress that sentence enough. If you are not strong and centered in your own mind, body, and spirit connection crystal healing for animals could be a struggle for you until you reach this point. It is about knowing who you are through your physical body, your higher self, as well as your own personal connection with Spirit, whether that is believing in God, Buddha, the Ultimate Being, a Divine Essence, a Universal Spirit, or whatever you choice of phrasing is for this higher power.

Let me explain a bit more about how the communication and relations between humans and animals work. An animal's mind can grasp and understand basic feelings as happiness, love, fear, and sadness. Animals work with **basic** feelings. Their mental wiring is not equipped for complex emotions and feelings such as guilt or blame. Animals function in a simpler fashion, working with the components of possible and impossible, not right or wrong. They live in the present moment, the NOW. Humans, on the other hand, work with intricate and complex designs. We work through an entire realm and spectrum of feelings, including the basics of happiness, love, fear, and sadness. However, we also deal with the emotional attributes of complexity too with such issues as guilt, blame, contempt, awe, disappointment, or optimism. Our mental and emotional wiring is set up differently, so we have to understand this basic concept before entering into a healing session with an animal.

For the physical ailment side, a human's mind is unlike that of an animal's mind when responding to these issues. Humans relate to pain. An animal reacts to pain. When I say humans relate to pain, this means that we can give an account or tell about the pain. We can tell someone where it hurts, how it hurts, what we are experiencing, and so on. When I say an animal reacts to pain, this means that they will react in response to the altercation causing this. This is one of the most important reasons to have a balanced mind, body, and spirit connection when approaching crystal healing for animals.

You have probably read or heard somewhere that certain animals can sense fear too. This is another important factor in working with crystal healing and animals. When you hold fear within yourself when working on any kind of healing task, whether it is for a human or an animal, this will be a big obstacle to overcome. However, when working with animals in particular, the fear can be sensed by the animals and even amplified by the crystal work you are trying to do.

Fear is a basic feeling, and animals can sense this in their own life, other animals, and in humans, whether we are performing a healing session or not. When you approach the animal companion for a healing, especially if you are using crystal healing as a basis for your work, you have to remove all fear on all levels before starting. To remove fear before starting a healing session, work on your own energy levels and issues dealing with fear. You can incorporate Agate into your own healing work before you begin a session. Make sure you cleanse, charge, and program a single piece of Agate to balance out your fear issues. Make sure you wear or keep this on you during all of your healing sessions to remove fear for the work. Because this is programmed for your energy and fear issue, this will not interfere with the animal healing session or other crystals that you would use. Please remember though, due to the amplification effect of crystal healing with fear issues, it is always best to start off slowly and gradually with healing sessions until you can learn to read the animals own communication with you and your higher self.

There are many ways to help heal our animal companions and use complimentary resources along with traditional medical care through a veterinarian. Crystal healing is just one of the many different ways you can work with your these special animals, whether they are your own animal companions or ones that you are providing a service for. You can also incorporate energy healing, sound/vibrational healing, herbal remedies, acupuncture, homeopathy, massage, hydrotherapy, and many other alternative therapies to help heal the ailments our animal companions face every day.

Just remember, by going into a session with a strong mind, body, spirit connection, and including the appropriate crystals, programmed and charged, and using the best intentions for all will produce a successful healing session, not only for the animal companion but yourself as well.

CHAPTER 5:
ANIMAL SIGNS

Working with animals can be an enjoyable part of anyone's practice, especially when you have a deep passion for them. They are living things, just as you and I are, and have feelings, physical pain, and underlying ailments that need our help too. Since we do not speak the same language, what can happen is a mental blockage builds up from within that can interfere in the way we communicate with these animals. Animal communication is a wonderful art that anyone can develop, but it all starts with being open, aware, and paying attention to the animal's signs that are right in front of us.

Let me demonstrate this on a human and physical level. If your leg was hurting, you could tell someone about this issue by using your voice, sign language, writing, or other techniques. Our animal companions cannot, but what they can do is show **tell-tail** signs of their physical ailments, especially if they are from injuries of physical issues. Understanding the physical issues is only a very small part of this work, along with learning to understand emotional issues, abuse, trauma signs, and much more. This book is not about animal communication, as that would be a whole other topic to write about, but what I am referring to is paying attention, opening your awareness, and noticing these signs even before you start your crystal healing process.

When working with animals, you may not always know what is wrong with them, especially if they are not your own pets. You may come across a stray cat or dog, or get called to help with an emergency and not really know the whole underlying cause. You begin by first paying attention to the animal's signs as they are presented to you before you even pick up a crystal and approach the animal. You have to notice the breathing, emotional status, if the animal is upset, fearful, physically hurt, or maybe they look as if they are crying on the inside. All of these things must be taken into an account even before you start. Why? This is a general rule of thumb for any kind of work, for both humans and animals alike. You would not want a doctor to prescribe medicine for you without knowing what was going on within your physical body. This is the same for animals, as you want to access the situation on all levels before choosing the crystals that you will begin with.

In most cases, you will know exactly what is wrong with the animal, whether it is your own pet or a friend/relatives pet, so this does make the healing process a bit easier. They can tell you that their precious one has been favoring his/her hind leg, has ear mites, or was diagnosed by their vet with a particular issue. This is a wonderful starting point, but you still need to pay attention to the animal's behavior before beginning. I cannot stress this enough! Our animal companions cannot verbally tell us if what we are doing is helping them or if they want more energy or maybe they want us to stop. They cannot sit up and say, "Please move the crystal a little bit further down my back" or "Can you move that away from my skin a

bit as it is really warm and uncomfortable at this time."
So it is up to us, following our intuition, and being aware of the animal we are working on to see how they are beforehand, during, and after the sessions.

I would like to jump into some of the signs that animals show during the sessions to let you know what you are doing is either successful or if you need to change something with your crystal healing process.
Remember every animal is different, just as we are, so these are good guidelines to go by. Keep a watchful eye on each animal, even if you have worked crystal healing on his/her energy levels before.

Positive signs of your crystal sessions can be anything from simple changes in behavior issues to major signs too. One of the key overlooked positive signs in crystal healing for animals is just the animal's positive attention. The animal will sit or lie next to the work that is being done and will just relax. Remember they work on simple basic mental and emotional wiring, they do not need to perform back flips to let you know that they enjoy the healing. Some of the basic sings for dogs, cats, and horses can be physical signs of comfort and affection such as wagging his/her tail in a relaxed and calm manner, drooling, muscles loosening and relaxing, sighing, eye-lids relaxing and closing, or nuzzling. These are not the only positive response signs you will see from the animals you work on, but are generally the most common.

You also have to remember that crystal healing energies, for animals, can integrate into their systems sometimes to quickly and this can be overwhelming for the animal. Animal's energy fields, even larger animals, are still a simple energetic structure and the energy work, whether this is from crystal healing or another form of healing, integrates within their energy fields very quickly. What may take a human's energy field thirty minutes to integrate may only take an animal's energy field five to ten minutes to integrate. This is helpful information, again, for making decisions about placing crystals on an animal's collar or harness. It is best to work slowly and introduce them one or two at a time. This concept also applies to a basic healing for any issue. If the energy starts to integrate to quickly into the energy fields, the animals will start to respond in a negative fashion. Some key warning signs for these are frantic tail wagging or thumping, foot stamping, clawing, hair-raising, showing his/her teeth, trying to avoid the crystal, growling, hissing, or biting. These, again, are just some of the warning signs, so please watch each animal closely during every session.

There is one more thing that many practitioners will do, and it is a common mistake when first starting out with crystal healing and animal work. When working with humans or animals, if you are working with specific crystals for a particular purpose behind the intention, please do not force the issue. This is generally done when we go against out gut feeling, intuition, and knowing when something isn't right. A good example of this is when you are working with your crystals and animals, and the crystals happen to slide and roll off the animal. Many practitioners, in the beginning, will say it is because the crystal or stone is an odd shape and does not lie flat. There are no perfectly shaped crystals and stones, whether they are natural or polished, that will lie exactly flat and not move unless they are specifically cut this way, and most are not.

When working on a crystal healing session, and a crystal is placed on the animals back while he/she is resting, and the crystal rolls off, what do you do? Most people would say to pick it up and put it back where it belongs, right? Yes the first time, and maybe even the second time too, depending on the shape and size of the crystal. However, if you are working with an animal session and the crystal keeps rolling off, there is a reason for this! It is not due to the crystal's size, shape, edges, or anything else. It is because the animal being worked on is not resonating within the vibrational match for that particular crystal at that time. That doesn't mean the crystal won't help heal, and it doesn't mean you are doing anything wrong. ***It simply means it is not meant for that particular crystal to be used at that place for that reason at that given moment in time.*** But does this mean every time a crystal rolls off that it is not resonating for that animal? No, this rule of thumb only applies to crystals that have rolled or slid off repeatedly during a single healing session.

Crystals will shift and move, as will the animal, but if they happen to do this more than twice, try considering an alternative crystal for this place or simply work on another area for the healing session. If this happens for multiple animals that you are working on, you should start over from the basics again. This could possibly be a simple fix as the crystals need to be thoroughly and deeply cleansed, followed by a re-programming and a re-charging of them for their own particular uses.

The same rule applies to crystals that are worn or placed for grid sessions. I have seen clients get animal pendants and collars for their pets and they chew each and every single one they tried to put on all because of the crystal they placed in it. They would say it is the animal that doesn't like the collar being there or the crystal is within reach. They would go out and purchase the exact same crystal and place it there again, and the same thing would happen. However, when the crystal was thoroughly cleansed, re-programmed, and re-charged for this healing area the animal left it alone.

If the crystal has been thoroughly cleansed, programmed, and charged and the animal is still trying to chew at it or refuses to be around the crystal, than it is a simple fix. The animal and crystal are just not

Practical Crystal Healing

resonating within the vibrational frequencies at that time. It isn't the collar, harness, medicine bag, or bedding.

Just as with people, animals vibrate at different frequency levels and what will work for one animal may not always work for all animals around the globe. The crystal tips in this book will work for the majority of animals the greater part of the time, no matter where they live or what circumstances they are surrounded with, as it is about balancing the energy they have within their own energetic fields that make up who he/she is in our life as an animal companion. So, if this happens to you or your animal companion, change the crystal instead of forcing the issue with them. Both you and your animal companion will be grateful that you did!

Chapter 6:
Animal Chakra Centers

Animals, just as humans, have chakra points located throughout their physical body. However, animals have 8 major chakra centers, 21 minor chakras, and 6 bud chakra points. Chakras centers for the majority of animals are located in the same areas, allowing for size ranges of the animals given larger or smaller, from a tiny little hamster to a large full-grown horse and everything in-between.

An animal's major chakra centers are dealing with the same kind of issues that we as humans work through with our major seven chakras, but they also have one major chakra center called the Brachial Chakra. This additional chakra center is a main energy point that links directly to all of the seven major chakra points as a whole. The Brachial Chakra serves as a connection point to human bonding and interaction too.

Animals also have minor chakra centers, some of which are used for healing purposes, such as the Primary Sensory Chakra, the six Bud Chakras, and a few others located throughout his/her body. The Primary Sensory Chakra is located on the bridge of the animal's nose, below the Third Eye/Brow Chakra center. The six Bud

Chakras are located on each foot, pad, paw, hoof, or claw, and one on the skin at the base opening of each ear. These chakra centers are receptive to even small energy vibrations and changes to help absorb and compute energetic frequencies to rely upon survival instincts. Using the sensitive vibrational readings through these minor chakras help animals determine impending danger and can flee. Bud Chakras located on the animal's foot, pad, paw, hoof, or claw can also help the animal ground its own energy with Mother Earth. These are similar to our human foot chakra counterparts.

Each chakra center has its own associative properties from crystals to colors, attributes, physical influences, emotional responses and much more. When working on a particular chakra center use the appropriate crystals listed as a guideline for the healing session.

Major Chakra Centers For Animals

1st – Root Chakra – Red Colored - Located at the base of the tail; where the tail meets the body of the animal. This chakra center deals with issues of security, being aware of the body, and physical survival. When this chakra center is not balanced an animal can show signs of being extremely fearful, aggression, sluggish, flight reactions, and restlessness. Crystals to be used for this chakra area are Hematite, Garnet, Red Jasper, and Ruby. To awaken and balance this chakra area, sit with the animal on Mother Earth and the appropriate crystals for a strong fluid energetic pathway.

2nd – Sacral Chakra – Orange Colored - Located near the lower abdomen area above the sexual organs. This chakra center deals with expression, emotional balance, control, and sexuality. When this chakra center is not balanced an animal can be overly emotional, have boundary issues, hormonal problems, and can be excessively vocal (barking, purring, whinnying, squawking, or hissing). Crystals to be used for this chakra area are Carnelian, Orange Calcite, and Coral. To awaken and balance this chakra, meditate with these crystals and the animal as you proceed through a guided visualization to see the chakra awakened, balanced, and physical health returning.

3rd – Solar Plexus Chakra – Yellow Colored - Located at the upper chest area, a few inches back from the front legs. This chakra center deals with the animal's sense of personal power, determination, assertion, and sense of self. When this chakra is not balanced, an animal can be perceived as apprehensive, overemphasis of power, dominating, or withdrawn. Crystals to be used for this chakra area are Citrine, Tiger's Eye, Golden Calcite, and Topaz. To awaken and balance this chakra area, rub the animal's upper belly area in a clockwise motion with the crystals in your dominant hand. Become aware of the radiating energy from this region.

4th – Heart Chakra – Green Colored (With pink coloration for stability in working with the minor Higher Heart Chakra) - Located in the front of the chest area. An alternative location for this chakra center is also located behind the forelegs on the upper chest area. This chakra center deals with relationships and the emotional connection established with them, unconditional love, balance, tolerance, forgiveness, compassion, and group consciousness. When this chakra is not balanced an animal will show signs of sadness, grief, jealously, overly possessive, self-centered, or be unwilling to interact with others. Crystals to be used for this chakra area are a combination of green and pink coloration for balance issues and to stabilize the energy centers, such as Emerald, Jade, Rose Quartz, and Pink Topaz. To awaken and balance these chakras, work with the animal and these crystals in an emotional environment, such as helping others or providing emotional support.

The animal's heart and higher heart chakras will respond to the energy you are resonating with and will awaken and balance in response to this.

5th – Throat Chakra – Blue Colored - Located at the upper throat area. This chakra center deals with communication aspects, expression, eloquence, and faith in the divine. When this chakra is not balanced, an animal will not communicate normally and become much less vocal, raspy, and have ego issues. Crystals to be used for this chakra area are Blue Quartz, Blue Topaz, Turquoise, and Aquamarine. To awaken and balance this chakra chant, hum, or sing with these crystals and the animal to bring a positive energetic connection and promote healing.

6th – Third Eye/Brow Chakra – Purple/Violet Colored - Located at the center of the forehead just above the eye area. This chakra center deals with acceptance on self, receiving guidance, spiritual energy, wisdom, intuition, and keen perception. When this chakra is not balanced an animal will appear to be distracted, experience headaches, and have physical issues concerning their eyes. Crystals to be used for this area are Fluorite, Amethyst, Blue Sapphire, and Lapis Lazuli. To awaken and balance this chakra, meditate with these crystals and the animal as you proceed through a guided visualization to see the chakra awakened, balanced, and physical health returning.

7th – Crown Chakra – Clear/White Colored - Located at the crown top of the head and between the ears. This chakra center deals with the animal's connection to Spirit and the Universal Source, cosmic consciousness, spirituality, and oneness with all. When this chakra is not balanced, the animal can appear depressed, withdrawn, feeling confined, and have intense anxiety issues. Crystals to be used for this area are Clear Quartz, Tanzanite, and Diamond. To awaken and balance this chakra, meditate with these crystals and the animal as you proceed through a guided visualization to see the chakra awakened, balanced, and physical health returning.

8th – Brachial Chakra – Located between the shoulders on the back. This chakra center is a link to all of the major chakras. It is also the chakra center for the connection between animal and human bonding. When working with chakra healing on your animal, or any general healing, this is the chakra center where you will need to start your healing. When this chakra is not balanced, the animal will not want to be touched, act withdrawn from healing, or have a refusal to connect for a session. Crystals to be used for this area are Black Tourmaline if the animal is reluctant to connect for a session or a Herkimer Diamond for a general healing of this area and connection to all major chakras. To awaken and balance this chakra, meditate with these crystals and the animal as you proceed through a guided visualization to see the chakra awakened, balanced, and physical health returning.

Primary Sensory Minor Chakra – Located at the bridge of the nose below the Third Eye/Brow Chakra. This chakra placement helps animals absorb and compute energetic frequencies to rely upon its own survival instincts. When this minor chakra is not balanced, the animal can show emotional signs of being lost, scattered, confused, or even off course. Crystals to be used for this area are Angelite and Rainbow Fluorite. To awaken and balance this chakra, slowly massage the area with one of these crystals for as long as the animal will allow.

Bud Chakras (Foot Area) – Located on the bottom of each foot, pad, paw, hoof, or claw. These chakra centers help animals ground and sense energy shifts. Crystals to be used for this area are Brown Carnelian or Jasper. To awaken and balance these chakras, slowly massage the area with one of these crystals for

Practical Crystal Healing

as long as the animal will allow. Be careful, as these areas are very sensitive when working with massage and crystal healing.

Bud Chakras (Ear Area) – Located on the skin at the base opening of each ear. These chakra centers help with the animal's ability to sense energy shifts too. Crystals to be used for this area are a combination of Amber and Clear Quartz. To awaken and balance these chakras, slowly massage the area with one of these crystals for as long as the animal will allow.

CHAPTER 7:
ANIMAL AURA LEVELS

Our animal counterparts also have their own aura levels. An aura field, or aura level, is an electromagnetic field that surrounds every living thing – plants, animals, and people! A human's aura field can extend anywhere from six inches to three feet per level, depending on which of the seven main aura levels you are referring to, out from the physical body. This includes above us, around us, and underneath us into the ground. An animal's aura field is very similar to that of a human's. Imagine an energy bubble around your animal companion. See this energy bubble, in your mind's eye, in an oval shape as close as it can be without touching the animal. This is your animal's first aura level or field. Each field after this is surrounding the smaller one(s) until you have seen all seven main aura levels.

Animal aura fields show stagnant, blocked, or rip energy areas just as ours do. These can manifest from spiritual, emotional, mental and physical issues into our aura fields and can change all the time. Issues within the animal's aura fields are the first things that will show up when a trauma or illness has occurred.

The constant state of change in an aura level can be hard to detect if you do not know what you are looking for. However, once an animal becomes ill or has a traumatic event happen, these issues will remain in their aura fields until they are resolved. An animal that is positive, happy, and energetic will have much brighter and stronger aura level. One that is depressed, sadden, ill, or hurt will have weaker and a more dull appearance and feel to their aura levels. It is always good to remember the basics though, so when working with aura fields you have to remember the further you move away from the physical body the thinner the field will be.

To perform aura healing sessions on animal companions, remember that you do not have to be right next to the animal to make this connection. As long as you are within their aura field, and using the correct crystal for a particular issue the healing will take place. Beginning a session, you want to make sure you have a clear head, open heart, and have grounded your energy. You will begin by making large sweeping motions over the animal's aura layers with the appropriate crystal(s). A similar technique is applying the same methods before you begin and choosing your crystals, but this time instead of large sweeping motions, you can use a method of drawing the energy down with a similar brushing motion. An example would be that of brushing a dog, cat, or horse. This motion will help draw any of the negative and stagnant energy to the lower areas of the aura levels to be released into Mother Earth's energetic field.

Major Aura Levels For Animals

Aura Alignment – Use Citrine to align all aura levels. This, again, is like the bubble picture. If one bubble shifts, than this can disturb the other bubbles in alignment. A general aura alignment session with

Citrine will align all aura levels for the animal and bring about a harmonious and strong aura field.

Aura Cleansing - Use Lapis Lazuli to provide a general basic aura cleansing for all animals. This cleansing will cleanse and reach all levels that are in need.

Aura Protection - Use Labradorite to protect and cushion the animal's aura needs. This can be used in a combination with a protection crystal healing for the animal for safety reasons too.

First Aura Level – Known as the physical aura body. This aura level displays physical sensations that have occurred within the body as reactions to issues, trauma, and events. Use Dalmatian Jasper to cleanse and heal the first level.

Second Aura Level - Known as the etheric aura body. This aura level displays emotions with respect to the animal's self and energy. Use Angelite to cleanse and heal the second level.

Third Aura Level - Known as the rational mind. This aura level works to understand a situation that the animal may encounter. Use Bloodstone to cleanse and heal the third level.

Fourth Aura Level - Known as the astral or emotional body. This aura level works with bonding issues and the interaction the animal has with people. Use Peridot and Rose Quartz to cleanse and heal the fourth level.

Fifth Aura Level - Known as the lower aura body. This aura level works with the divine energy from the soul. Use Carnelian to cleanse and heal the fifth level.

Sixth Aura Level - Known as the higher mental aura body. This aura level displays divine love. Use Turquoise to cleanse and heal the sixth level.

Seventh Aura Level - Known as the spiritual and intuitive aura body. This aura level helps to connect with the divine mind. Use Celestite to cleanse and heal the seventh level.

CHAPTER 8:
CRYSTAL PENDULUM DOWSING

Crystals and pendulums are a great combination to help aid in your work with animal healing. Crystal pendulum dowsing is using a crystal pendulum to be able to connect with your higher self and guides to give you the correct answer to a question. Pendulum dowsing has been around for a long time and has been used for many reasons, such as finding water, minerals, lost items, and even helping to diagnose issues.

The key to working with crystal pendulum dowsing is to find the crystal pendulum that resonates within your energy fields. Some people believe that you may need to use different pendulums for different reasons based on their energetic properties. This is not true. You may, if you so choose to, have different pendulums and use them for different reasons, but it is not required. What is best is to go out and find one that you are drawn to, similar to working with your intuition and choosing your crystals. Your pendulum will choose you just as much as you choose it, so the best advice is to keep it simple and trust in your higher self when choosing your crystal pendulum.

After you have chosen your pendulum, you will want to become familiar with how this works. What happens during a crystal pendulum dowsing session is that you connect to your higher self and spirit guides, whomever you wish to call them, to get the best answer at that time to the question that is asked. Normally pendulum-dowsing sessions are done with simple "Yes" or "No" types of answers, but they can also be intended to spell out words. What I am going to describe here for you is a simple "Yes" or "No" technique that anyone can do with a crystal pendulum if you choose to use this in aiding you with your animal healing sessions.

First, you will need to cleanse your new pendulum before starting the programming or asking questions. Just as the store bought crystals you use during your healing sessions, crystal pendulums can collect energetic debris that has to be cleansed before using. You have no idea who was handling the pendulum before you or if they were asking it questions or playing with them at the store. It is best to perform a simple cleansing of this before you begin. You can use any of the cleansing techniques that were discussed in Chapter 2. Smudging and water cleansing are the easiest and quickest ones to use for pendulum sessions.

Once your crystal pendulum is cleansed, you will need to program this so you can read the answers for each question you ask. To do this, hold the pendulum in your dominant hand and make an energetic connection with the crystal. When you are ready, hold the chain or cord of the pendulum and allow the crystal pendulum to come to a complete stop by gently tapping the tip on the palm of your hand. Close your eyes and ask it to show you how it will move for a "Yes" answer. It may swing side-to-side, up and down, clockwise circles or counter-clockwise circles. Whatever the movement is, take note that this means a "Yes" answer.

Now stop the crystal by gently tapping the tip again on the palm of your hand. Ask it this time how it will move for a "No" answer. Again, it may swing in side-to-side, up or down, clockwise, or counter-clockwise circles. Just take note of which way it is swinging for a "No" answer. Repeat both the "Yes" and "No" answer questions one more time to make sure you understand both movements before starting your crystal pendulum dowsing. You may also ask it test questions, such as confirming your name, age, or any other yes or no answer types of questions to get practice working with your pendulum.

Crystal pendulum dowsing for animals can be performed either in person or via distant sessions if you have a picture of the animal you are working with. Remember you want to ask "Yes" or "No" types of questions when working with this to make sure you get the correct answers and results. You can start by asking if the animal's name is correct and by asking if the animal is a dog (or cat, horse, bird, etc) to make sure you connection is accurate before starting in with other questions. Work through all of the questions that you have to narrow down the topic that is causing the animal's ailment. This may be a physical, mental, emotional, or spiritual type of issue, so work through your intuition and keep asking questions until you find the source.

An in-person crystal pendulum dowsing session can be done in the same manner with "Yes" and "No" types of answers. When you want to check for a painful physical spot on the animal, you can ask the pendulum to swing in the "Yes" manner when it is over the area of concern. You can also use this technique for underlying ailments, such as problems with internal organs or emotional issues.

Practical Crystal Healing

If you receive a negative response after going over the entire animal's physical body, cleanse and program your crystal pendulum again. You will want to care for your crystal pendulum in the same manner that you care for your healing crystals. The pendulums are here to serve as a way of communicating with your higher self and intuition in aiding with your animal healing sessions. They are still crystals and need your love and care to maintain them just as much as your healing kits do. Their function is a bit different in your healing pathway, but they still serve a purpose and use their energy to help with your connections on a subconscious level.

Chapter 9: Crystal Healing Kits For Animals

Just as you have crystal-healing bags for yourself or your healing practice, you will want to keep one for your animal companion work too. Here are some guidelines for a basic all purpose animal healing kit, as well as customized healing kits for the different animals you may encounter. Different animals respond well to different crystals, especially dealing with "on the spot" healing sessions, so it is good to make sure you have the basics as well as the others you will be working on in the future. I refer to them as the staples to have around when working with animals and healing, similar to band-aids in a first aid kit.

Basic Animal Healing Kit

Make sure you have crystals that correspond with either the chakras, auras, or color references if you are working with just one basic healing kit. Good staples to have on hand for on the spot healings are: Amber, Amethyst, Aquamarine, Carnelian, Citrine, Clear Quartz, Emerald, Fluorite, Garnet, Hematite,

Malachite, Onyx, Rose Quartz, Smoky Quartz, and Turquoise.

Animal Healing Kit For Dogs
Amethyst, Carnelian, Clear Quartz, Lapis Lazuli, Obsidian, Peridot, Red Jasper, and Yellow Jasper.

Animal Healing Kit For Cats
Celestite, Fluorite, Malachite, Moonstone, Orange Calcite, Ruby, Smoky Quartz, and Tiger's Eye.

Animal Healing Kit For Horses
Aquamarine, Black Obsidian, Citrine, Fluorite, Garnet, Rhodonite, Tiger's Eye, and Turquoise.

Animal Healing Kit For Birds
Amber, Bloodstone, Brown Carnelian, Jasper, Onyx, Smoky Quartz, Sodalite and Tanzanite.

Animal Healing Kits For Reptiles
Apache Tears, Carnelian, Clear Quartz, Hematite, Obsidian, Petalite, Red Jasper, and Turquoise.

Animal Healing Kit For Wildlife
Black Tourmaline, Brown Carnelian, Clear Quartz, Jasper, Moonstone, Moss Agate, Red Jasper, and Tree Agate.

Some of the techniques and tips may require using more than one crystal at a time, or using other crystals that are not shown in these above listings. These are meant to give you a good variety of different healing kit combinations that you can use in your own animal companion healing work. This offers a variety of good crystals and stones to get you started, as well as have on hand when emergencies or ailments do arise. These are all wonderful vibrational matches for our animal companions. I recommend starting with these, and then adding to your collection as you wish.

There are also some crystals and stones out in the world that you need to become familiar with because of their harmful toxins in which they were created. Just because the crystals and stones carry an element within them that is harmful, if ingested, does not mean it doesn't have major potential for healing purposes. They need to be taken care of properly especially when using them for healing issues, attaching them to an animal's collar/harness, grid placement, and when making elixirs and mists.

When working with animals and these crystals, you will also need to make sure that the crystals are out of the animal's reach. Some of these tips and techniques may require having a crystal attached to the animal's collar or harness. You will want to make sure that the crystal is attached securely and that the animal cannot chew, bite, lick, or swallow the crystal. The same principle applies to crystals that are placed around the animal or area for grid placement as our animal companions are very curious about these living rocks and love to feel their energy. They do not know or understand that these are not to be ingested and may possibly be harmful to them if they start chewing on them! Elixirs and mists should have extra precautions taken as to not provide anything harmful to the animal you are working with. When using these crystals and stones for elixirs or mists, you should only use one of the indirect crystal charges described in Chapter 3.

A good rule of thumb is to be extra careful and double check the crystals and stones that may contain aluminum, arsenic, chlorine, copper, iron, lead, mercury, sulphur, zinc, or any other harmful toxins. Polished stones are less likely to cause harm as compared to some natural pieces. I am not an expert geologist, nor do I know all of the chemical components of these beautiful crystals. ***I am, however, an expert spiritual healer and know how to use them for healing purposes.*** Therefore, I have written this book on healing with crystals and not a chemical composition of their make-ups. For more information about a particular crystal, please research its general chemical components. In addition, as always, remember that they are apart of Mother Earth's beauty and are here, not to harm, but to help in everyway they can!

Chapter 10:
555 Crystal Healing Tips & Techniques

All of the 555 tips and techniques listed in this chapter are meant for the use of our animal companions – for dogs, cats, horses, birds, fish, reptiles, and many more. The ailment/issue that needs to be addressed, along with the appropriate crystal(s) to be used, is listed in alphabetical order for each technique. Make sure to double check, when creating elixirs and mists, that you use an appropriate method for each individual crystal, as you can refer back to Chapter 3 for the different crystal charging methods. When securing crystals to an animal's harness, collar, cage, or crate make sure they are secure to the area and cannot be chewed, bitten, or swallowed. Proper securing of these crystals is key when leaving them around the animal for long periods of time. Animals are very curious, so for the safety of all concerned, make sure you double-check everything!

ABANDONMENT ISSUES – Use Rhodonite for a healing session, as close to the animal's heart chakra as possible, for a 20-minute time period over five days.

ABSCESS – Make sure to use hypoallergenic tape, and securely tape Petrified Palm Wood to the area for a minimum of four days.

ABUSED – Hold a piece of Pink Tourmaline over the higher heart chakra for a 20-minute healing session for a seven-day period and repeat as necessary. You can also have the animal wear a programmed Pink Tourmaline on the collar/harness as close to the higher heart chakra as possible.

ACNE - Make an Amethyst gem elixir, charging for 2 hours, and gently rinse the areas that are affected by this issue twice a day.

ACUTE STRESS SYNDROME – Attach Peridot and Pink Topaz to the animal's collar/harness around the heart chakra area and have them wear this continually for best results. Cleanse every 30 days!

ADDISON'S DISEASE – Perform a 15 minute crystal healing session using Aventurine and Black Tourmaline every day to help decrease the issues dealing with this disease.

ADJUSTMENT PERIOD – Surround the crate/cage with Hematite and Pink Tourmaline for adjusting to a new home, family, or environment. He/she can also wear this crystal combination attached to the top of his/her collar or harness.

AFFECTION – Attach a Watermelon Tourmaline to the top of the animal's collar/harness for a minimum of 7 days to bring about a more affectionate energy.

AFRAID OF PEOPLE – Place a Black Tourmaline in your dominant hand and slowly work through the brachial chakra to help release this issue.

AGGRESSIVENESS (GENERAL) - Attach a Blue Lace Agate to the animal's collar/harness near the heart chakra for this behavioral issue. Cleanse and program this for aggression issues every 30 days.

AGGRESSIVE AT FEEDING TIME - Attach a Red Jasper to the underside of the animal's feeding bowl before each feeding session. Make sure this is cleansed, programmed and attached securely.

AGGRESSIVE TOWARDS PETTING – Make sure the person who is working with the animal holds Halite in his/her dominant hand before working with the animal. Once the animal responds in a calm fashion, switch hands and pet the animal with the dominant hand and hold the Halite in your opposite hand.

AGILITY – For agility issues, make sure you attach a piece of Green Jade to the animal's collar/harness over his/her back area for best results.

AIR SAC MITES – Attach Amber and Bloodstone to the underside of the bird's cage for a minimum of seven days.

AIR TRAVEL – Make a Hematite gem elixir, using an indirect method and charging for 1 hour. Place five drops on the animal's tongue before air travel time. You can also secure a piece of Hematite to the animal's crate, cage, harness, or collar during air travel periods.

ALCOHOL – For alcohol consumption, use a Turquoise and Hematite combination over the stomach area for a 30-minute session.

AMPUTATION CONCERNS – During the recovery time, securely attach a piece of Amber to the animal's cage/crate. For long-term use, attach a programmed piece of Amber to the animal's collar/harness.

ANAL GLAND ISSUES – Use a Smoky Quartz, turning clockwise, around the area for 15 minutes to help work on anal gland issues.

ANCHOR WORM (FISH) – Attach a Ruby and Apatite combination to the outside of the aquarium for a minimum of seven days.

ANEMIA – Make a gem elixir of Hematite and Bloodstone, charging 1 hour, and place a few drops in the animal's water every day or directly on his/her tongue once a day.

ANIMAL FIGHTING – Make a gem elixir of Black Tourmaline and Peridot, charging for 30 minutes, and give every animal that is concerned with the fighting issue 5 drops on his/her tongue.

ANTI-SOCIAL ISSUES – Attach a Lapis Lazuli to the animal's collar/harness as close as you can to the throat chakra area for best results.

ANXIETY (GENERAL) – Attach a Peridot to the collar/harness as close as you can to the heart chakra. Cleanse and re-program every 14 days.

ANXIETY DURING CAR TRAVEL – Secure a Moonstone and Hematite to the top of the animal's cage, crate, collar, or harness during car traveling sessions. You can also make a gem elixir, charging for 1 hour, and place 5 drops on the animal's tongue before traveling.

APPETITE CHANGE – Charge the animal's food with a combination of Tiger's Eye and Carnelian by holding the crystal combination over the food and turning the crystals in a clockwise motion for 5 minutes before feeding.

APPETITE STIMULATION – Charge the animal's food with Carnelian by holding the crystal over the food and turning the crystal in a counter-clockwise motion for 5 minutes before feeding.

APPLE SEEDS – For apple seed consumption, place Turquoise and Black Tourmaline over the stomach area and turn the crystals clockwise for 10 minutes.

APRICOT/CHERRY/PEACH PITS – For apricot/cherry/peach pit consumption, place Zircon and Black Tourmaline near the animal's stomach and allow the animal to rest and absorb the energies for as long as they will permit.

AQUARIUM CLEARING – Place a Clear Quartz in your dominant hand and a Moonstone in your opposite hand and slowly turn them counter-clockwise around the entire aquarium's perimeter.

ARTHRITIS (DEGENERATIVE JOINT DISEASE) – Make a Rainbow Fluorite gem elixir, charging for 3 hours, and gently mist all areas that are affecting the animal or all joints in general from head to toe. You can also bathe the animal in the charged water for a full body session.

ASTHMA – Attach a programmed Tiger's Eye to the underside of the animal's collar/harness. Remember to cleanse and re-program every 30 days.

ATTACKING ANKLES – Make a Tanzanite and Watermelon Tourmaline gem elixir, charging for 30 minutes, and gently mist the animal every time they try to attack someone's ankles.

ATTACKING BEHAVIOR (GENERAL) – Securely attach Barite to the animal's collar near the throat chakra for best results. Cleanse and re-program every 30 days.

ATTENTION SEEKING – Make a gem elixir of Jade and Rose Quartz, charging for 30 minutes, and place 5 drops on your animal's tongue 3 times a day.

AVOCADO – For avocado consumption, place Black Tourmaline and Clear Quartz over his/her stomach area and turn the crystals clockwise for 10 minutes.

BACK PROBLEMS – When the animal is calm, place one piece of Petrified Wood on each side of the back area and an Onyx near his/her tail and allow the healing to take place for 15 minutes.

BACK SCRATCHING – Hold a Botswana Agate near the area of scratching and turn this clockwise for 15 minutes. You can also make a gem elixir with Botswana Agate, charging for 30 minutes, and gently mist the area he/she is scratching.

BACTERIAL GILL DISEASE (FISH) – Attach Sodalite and Clear Quartz to the outside of the aquarium for a minimum of 7 days.

BAD BREATH – Make a Carnelian and Amber gem elixir, charging for 1 hour, and place 5 drops on the animal's tongue or 10 drops in the animal's drinking water daily.

BAD DREAMS – Place Jasper and Emerald surrounding the animal's cage/crate during sleep time. You can also make a gem elixir, charging for 1 hour, and gently mist the animal's head right after falling sleeping.

BAIT – A gem elixir of Clear Quartz and Onyx, charged for 1 hour, misted onto the bait will help prevent aggression towards biting it off the hook!

BALANCE PROBLEMS – Attach Blackstar to the animal's collar/harness for working on balance issues. Cleanse and re-program every 30 days.

BALANCING ANIMAL ENERGIES – Use Moss Agate and thoroughly cleanse the animal's aura for the balancing of his/her energies.

BALD SPOTS – Make an Amethyst and Snowflake Obsidian gem elixir, charging for 1 hour, and gently mist the bald spot areas on the animal's coat/fur.

BAREBACK RIDING – Securely attach Rhodonite and Jade to the horse for working with bareback riding issues.

BARKING (EXCESSIVE) – Cleanse, program, and attach an Aquamarine to the animal's collar/harness near the throat chakra.

BEAK PROBLEMS (BIRD) – Make a Sodalite gem elixir, charging for 30 minutes, and drench a cotton-ball with the charged water. Gently pat the bird's beak twice a day.

BEDDING (ENERGETIC CLEANSING) – Create a Topaz gem elixir, charging for 2 hours, and gently mist all bedding areas that the animal rests in. This can be a cage, crate, animal bed, stable, and outside housing.

BEGGING – Cleanse and program an Emerald to keep on hand when the animal starts begging. Hold this in your dominant hand and tell them "No." This will become easier each time you use this crystal!

BIRD CLAWS (GENERAL) – Use a combination of Onyx and Jasper in a gem elixir, charging for 1 hour, and either gently mist the bird's claws or drench a cotton-ball and gently pat his/her claws with the charged water.

BIRD MITES – Make an indirect charged gem elixir with Hematite, charging for 1 hour, and gently mist the entire cage, area, bird, and surroundings to help eliminate bird mites.

BITE WOUNDS – Hold Carnelian and Celestite in your dominant hand and turn clockwise around the bite wound for 15 minutes.

BITING BEHAVIOR (GENERAL) – Cleanse, program, and securely attach an Aquamarine and Hematite combination to the animal's collar/harness to help heal general biting issues.

BITS (HORSE) - Create an Aquamarine gem elixir, charging for 1 hour, and generously mist the bit before putting this in the horse's mouth.

BITING BARK OFF TREES – Make a Tree Agate and Jasper gem elixir, charging for 1 hour, and gently mist all of the trees that the animal has access to, whether they have bitten the bark off or not. You can also attach this programmed crystal combination securely to the animal's collar/harness.

BLADDER ISSUES – Hold a Carnelian and Citrine in your dominant hand and slowly work in clockwise circles over the animal's bladder area for a 10-minute session.

BLEEDING (GENERAL) – Place Bloodstone, surrounding the area of concern, for 15 minute time periods. Cleanse thoroughly afterwards.

BLEEDING FROM THE MOUTH – Place Bloodstone and Aquamarine surrounding the mouth, one on each side if possible, and allow the crystal energies to be absorbed by the animal.

BLEEDING FROM THE RECTUM – Place Bloodstone and Red Jasper surrounding the rectum area, one on each side if possible, and allow the crystal energies to be absorbed by the animal.

BLINDNESS – Cleanse, program, and securely attach an Onyx and Opal to the animal's collar/harness. Cleanse and re-program every 30 days to help deal with this issue.

BLISTER DISEASE (REPTILES) – Make a Clear Quartz, Citrine, and Turquoise gem elixir, charging for 1 hour, and place 15 drops into the animal's water, or 5 drops on its tongue.

BLISTERS (GENERAL) – Make an Aquamarine and Carnelian gem elixir, charging for 1 hour, and gently mist or pat the blistered area.

BLOATING – Place a Golden Topaz in your dominant hand slowly turn this counter-clockwise over the bloated area three times a day for 7 days.

BOARDING ISSUES – Cleanse, program, and securely attach a combination of Lapis Lazuli and Clear Quartz to the animal's collar/harness for the boarding time period. Afterwards remove and cleanse thoroughly.

BOLTING OUT DOORS – Make sure you have two Smoky Quartz and two Tiger's Eye's for this issue. Securely attach one combination of a Smoky Quartz and Tiger's Eye to the animal's collar/harness and place one Smoky Quartz and one Tiger's Eye by the door that they bolt out of. Make sure to cleanse all four crystals every 30 days.

BONDING ISSUES – Use Leopardskin Jasper and thoroughly cleanse the aura field of the animal and the human that is trying to bond with them. Then work on making a connection through the brachial chakra using the Leopardskin Jasper.

BONE ISSUES (GENERAL) – Place Apatite surrounding the animal, when they are in a calm and resting state, and allow the healing to transpire for 15 minutes, or as long as the animal will allow.

BOREDOM – Make a gem elixir with Lepidolite, charging for 20 minutes, and gently mist the animal and the general surroundings to release boredom issues.

BOTS (HORSES) – Make a Hematite and Turquoise gem elixir, charging for 1 hour, and generously mist the animal from head to tail.

BOUNDARIES – Program Barite for the boundary issues you want the animal to understand and securely attach this to the animal's collar/harness.

BOWEL ISSUES (GENERAL) – Surround the animal with Yellow Jasper and Topaz, in a circle formation, and allow the crystal energies to heal the animal at 15-minute intervals.

BOWEL OBSTRUCTION – Place Citrine in your dominant hand and place Pyrite in opposite hand. Gently move in clockwise motions around the lower abdomen of the animal for 20-minute intervals, three times a day.

BRAIN INJURY – Attach Amazonite and Green Tourmaline to the top of the animal's collar/harness near the injury. Cleanse and re-program every 7 days.

BREATHING DIFFICULTY – Hold a Blue Topaz and Hematite in your dominant hand and work slowly around the animal's chest area in counter-clockwise motions.

BREATHLESSNESS (BIRD) – Secure Copper and Amber to the underside of the bird's cage for a minimum of 7 days to help with breathlessness issues.

BREEDING ISSUES (GENERAL) – Attach a Bloodstone to the underside of the animal's collar/harness, as close as you can to his/her mid-abdomen area for best results.

BRITTLE NAILS – Make an Obsidian gem elixir, charging for 1 hour, and generously mist the brittle nails as much as the animal will allow.

BROCCOLI (EXCESSIVE AMOUNTS) - For broccoli consumption, use a Hematite and Carnelian combination over the stomach area for a 30-minute session.

BRONCHITIS – Hold an Aquamarine in your dominant hand and turn the crystal clockwise over the chest area for 15-minute intervals up to five times a day.

BRUSHING – Hold the grooming brush in your dominant hand and hold Peridot in your opposite hand while you are brushing the animal. Make sure to have the crystal close to the animal so he/she can feel the energy effects from the crystal and through your own energy connection with this.

BUCKING – Attach a combination of Carnelian and Amethyst to the horse's reins before riding to help calm down bucking issues.

BULLYING PROBLEMS – Attach a Blue Tourmaline to the animal's collar/harness near the heart chakra. Cleanse and re-program the crystal every 14 days.

BUMBLE FOOT (BIRD) – Attach a Brown Carnelian to the underside of the bird's cage for 30 days. For an alternative, make a Brown Carnelian gem elixir, charging for 30 minutes, and generously mist the area twice a day for 14 days.

BURNS – Make a Chrysoprase gem elixir, charging for 20 minutes, and lightly mist the area that is burned three times a day.

BURSITIS – Hold a Blue Lace Agate and Azurite in your dominant hand and circle the areas of concern clockwise for 10 minute time periods.

BURYING BONES (EXCESSIVE) – Make a Golden Obsidian gem elixir, charging for 30 minutes, and lightly mist all of the unburied bones thoroughly. Allow them to dry before giving them back to the animal.

BURYING FOOD – Make a Howlite gem elixir, charging for 30 minutes, and lightly mist any food that is available to the animal's to help prevent burying issues.

CALMING/SOOTHING – Securely attach an Amethyst to the animal's collar/harness to bring about a calming and soothing energy.

CANCER – Hold Selenite in your dominant hand and slowly move the crystal clockwise around the animal's entire physical body once, and then return to the location of the cancer and turn the crystal counter-clockwise. The entire session can last about 10 minutes. Provide this session three times a day, or as often as the animal will allow.

CANDY CONTAINING XYLITOL – For candy consumption, use a Hematite and Amber combination over the stomach area for a 30-minute session.

CANNIBALISM – Attach Apache Tears to the animal's collar/harness or cage and allow the energies to work for 7 days in a row. Remove for 7 days, and repeat as needed.

CAR SICKNESS – Secure a Clear Quartz and Hematite to the top of the animal's cage, crate, collar, or harness during car traveling sessions. A gem elixir for these crystals can be made by charging the water for 1 hour. Place 5 drops on the animal's tongue before traveling.

CAT – BIRD AGGRESSION – Cleanse and program a Fire Agate for the cat and an Angelite for the bird to become energetic friends. Securely attach the Fire Agate to the cat's collar and securely attach the Angelite to the underside of the bird's cage. Cleanse and re-program every 30 days.

CAT NIP AGGRESSION (EXCESSIVE) – Make an Aqua Aura gem elixir, charging for 30 minutes, and lightly mist the catnip or toys.

CATARACTS – While the animal is calm, hold a Purple Fluorite near the animal's eye and third eye chakra. Make sure to move the crystal in a clockwise motion around the animal for 10-15 minutes, or as long as the animal will allow.

CHANGE (GENERAL) – Attach a combination of Rose Quartz and Sodalite to the animal's collar/harness to allow his/her energies to accept change and adjust.

CHARGING – Cleanse, program, and securely attach an Onyx and Rose Quartz combination to the animal's collar/harness to help take control of charging issues.

CHARGING BATH WATER – Cleanse, program, and securely attach a Clear Quartz and Rose Quartz to the animal's collar/harness to ease these issues.

CHASING CARS – Attach a combination of Carnelian and Amber to the animal's collar/harness to help ease the anxiety brought on by chasing cars.

CHASING OTHER ANIMALS (EXCESSIVE) – Attach a Golden Calcite to the animal's collar/harness to ease this issue.

CHASING TAIL – Make a Tiger's Eye and Carnelian gem elixir, charging for 1 hour, and gently mist the animal's tail and crown chakra.

CHERRY EYE – Hold a White/Cream Jade in your dominant hand and an Emerald in your opposite hand, and work slowly in clockwise circles around the area for 10 minutes three times a day.

CHEWING (EXCESSIVE) – Make a Clear Quartz and Turquoise gem elixir, charging for 30 minutes, and thoroughly mist the areas that the animal is chewing.

CHEWING CORDS – Make a Clear Quartz and Boji Stones gem elixir, charging for 30 minutes, and very lightly mist the areas of the cords that are covered entirely with the plastic sheath. Do not mist any open areas of cords!

CHEWING ON PAWS – Make a Brown Carnelian gem elixir, charging for 30 minutes, and thoroughly mist the animal's paws.

CHEWING ON TAIL – Make an Onyx and Smoky Quartz gem elixir, charging for 30 minutes, and thoroughly mist the animal's tail.

CHIGGER BITES – Make a Clear Quartz, Fire Agate, and Onyx gem elixir, charging for 1 hour, and thoroughly mist the entire area.

CHILDREN AND ANIMALS - Make sure you have enough Clear Quartz for all living things involved in this relationship. Program all of the crystals for the corresponding children and animal's to get along, and securely place them on a necklace for each child and attach one to each animal's collar/harness.

CHOCOLATE – For chocolate consumption, use a Bloodstone and Hematite combination over the stomach area and turn the crystals clockwise for 15-minute intervals.

CHRISTMAS TREE – For this issue, you will need to do two separate crystal healings. First, make a Black Tourmaline gem elixir, charging for 30 minutes, and thoroughly mist the base and trunk of the Christmas tree. Next, make a Tree Agate gem elixir, charging for 30 minutes, and gently mist the entire room the Christmas tree is residing in.

CHRONIC EGG LAYING – Make a Black Agate gem elixir, charging for 1 hour, and place 10 drops of the elixir in the animal's water or on it's food to help control this issue.

CIGARETTES/CIGARS/TOBACCO – For tobacco consumption, use a Golden Calcite and Garnet combination over the stomach area for a 30-minute session.

CINCH ITCHING – Use a Carnelian and Clear Quartz gem elixir, charging for 1 hour, and gently mist the entire area that is of concern.

CLAW OVERGROWTH – Make a Yellow Calcite and Brown Jasper gem elixir, charging for 1 hour, and thoroughly mist the claw overgrowth areas three times a day.

CLAWING – Use a Blue Lace Agate and Amethyst gem elixir, charging for 30 minutes, and gently mist all clawing areas of concern.

CLEANSE CARPET TOXINS – Place Malachite in the four corners of the room to remove carpet toxins. Cleanse after 7 days. If you cannot place Malachite where the animal will not get into this, make a gem elixir, charging for 1 hour, and thoroughly mist the carpet areas every 7 days.

CLICKER TRAINING – Make sure you hold a programmed Green Jade in your opposite hand when working with clicker training for increased results.

CLIMBING ISSUES – Attach Albite securely to the animal's collar/harness to work on climbing issues.

COCCIDIA – Make a Topaz, Turquoise, and Clear Quartz gem elixir, charging for 1 hour, and place 5 drops on the animal's tongue 5 times a day for 7 days to help control this issue.

COFFEE – For coffee consumption, use Hematite over the stomach area for a 30-minute session.

COGNITIVE DYSFUNCTION – Securely attach a Diamond to the animal's collar/harness, as close as you can to his/her head, and allow the energies to heal on a consistent basis.

COLIC – Make an Amazonite gem elixir, charging for 1 hour, and place 5 drops on the animal's tongue three times a day.

COLITIS – Place a Moonstone, Clear Quartz, and Jade surrounding the animal for a minimum of 15 minutes a day for 7 days to help control these issues.

COMMON COLD – Surround the animal with Topaz and hold one over his/her head for 15 minutes, or as long as the animal will allow.

COMMUNICATION – Communication gaps with animal's can be narrowed by having the owner wear Faden Quartz and having the animal wear Dalmatian Jasper. Make sure they are both programmed for communication issues and cleanse regularly.

COMPULSIVE BEHAVIOR – Program and securely attach Infinite to the animal's collar/harness to counteract compulsive behavior.

CONFRONTATION – Make a Rose Quartz and Moonstone gem elixir, charging for 1 hour, and gently mist the entire area, animal, and issues dealing with confrontation.

CONGESTION – Hold Morganite near the animal's chest and turn in a clockwise motion for 15 minutes, or as long as the animal will allow.

CONSTIPATION – Make a Clear Tourmaline gem elixir, charging for 2 hours, and place 5 drops on the animal's tongue to help with constipation issues.

CONVULSIONS – Surround the animal with a circle of Moonstone, Carnelian, and Calcite for convulsion issues.

CORNEAL ULCER – Use a Clear Quartz and an Aquamarine gem elixir, charging for 1 hour, and place 3 drops in the eye up to three times a day.

COTTON-MOUTH (FISH) – Program and attach Citrine to the aquarium tank for 14 days. Re-program and repeat as needed.

CRAMPS – While the animal is resting, place Clear Quartz on opposite sides of the abdomen and one Hematite above the abdomen. Turn the Hematite counter-clockwise for 10-minute intervals.

CRATE TRAINING – Surround the crate with securely attached pieces of Petrified Wood programmed to help with training purposes.

CUSHING'S DISEASE – Surround the animal with a circle of Sugilite and Clear Quartz twice a day for 15 minute time periods to ease the issues with this disease.

CUTS/SCRAPES – Make a Carnelian and Black Obsidian gem elixir, charging for 20 minutes, and gently mist the areas of concern. Allow them all to air dry.

CYSTIC STONES – Hold Garnet in your dominant hand and slowly move this in clockwise motions around the animal for 15 minutes at a time.

DANDRUFF – Make a Snowflake Obsidian and Green Jade gem elixir, charging for 1 hour, and gently mist the animal down from head to paw once a week.

DAY CARE ISSUES – Program and securely attach Prehnite to the animal's collar/harness before attending animal day care to keep anxiety and other issues under control.

DECLAW – Make sure your use hypoallergenic tape and securely tape a programmed Clear Quartz to the area for a minimum of five days.

DEGENERATIVE DISC DISEASE – Securely attach an Andean Opal and Citrine combination to the animal's collar/harness. Cleanse and re-program every 30 days.

DEHYDRATION – Make an Aquamarine gem elixir, charging for 30 minutes, and place 5 drops on the animal's tongue 5 times a day.

DENTAL PROBLEMS (GENERAL) – Create a Aquamarine and Fluorite gem elixir, charging for 30 minutes, and gently rub the elixir over the animal's gum line, place 5 drops on his/her tongue, or place 10 drops in the drinking water every day.

DEPIGMENTATION – Use a Clear Quartz, Rose Quartz, and Onyx gem elixir, charging for 1 hour, and bathe the animal in this charged water. Repeat every 7 days.

DEPRESSION – Perform a general crystal healing session using Amber around the entire physical body of the animal to decrease the issues with depression.

DEPTH PERCEPTION – Program and securely attach Fluorite to the animal's collar/harness when the animal has depth perception issues.

DERMATITIS – Make a Wavellite gem elixir, charging for 1 hour, and gently rinse the areas that are of concern twice a day.

DERMOID CYSTS – Use a Green Jade in a crystal healing session for this issue twice a day.

DESTRUCTIVE ANXIETY BEHAVIOR – Program and securely attach Howlite and Pink Tourmaline to the animal's collar/harness to calm down issues from this behavior.

DETACHED RETINA – Make a Rose Quartz and Tiger's Eye gem elixir, charging for 1 hour, and place 3 drops in the eye of concern three times a day.

DIABETES – Program and securely attach a Citrine to the animal's collar/harness and place a programmed Amethyst where the animal sleeps. Cleanse and re-program them every 30 days.

DIARRHEA – Use a Clear Quartz and Red Jasper gem elixir, charging for 30 minutes, and place 5 drops on the animal's tongue 5 times a day.

DIFFICULTY SWALLOWING – Securely attach an Aqua Aura to the animal's collar as close to the throat as possible. Cleanse every 7 days.

DIGESTION – Attach a programmed Labradorite to the animal's collar/harness. Next, make a Jasper gem elixir, charging for 30 minutes, and place 10 drops of this charged water on the animal's food before eating.

DIGGING HOLES (EXCESSIVE) – Make a Tiger's Eye and Peridot gem elixir, charging for 1 hour, and thoroughly mist all of the areas that the animal is digging in and any other areas to prevent future digging issues. You can also attach this programmed crystal combination securely to the animal's collar/harness.

DISLOCATED JOINTS – Securely attach an Azurite near the area of the dislocated joints for 14 days. Cleanse, re-program and attach again.

DISORIENTATION – Attach a Peridot to the back of your animal's collar/harness to help with disorientation issues. Cleanse and re-program every 14 days.

DISTEMPER – Surround the animal with Clear Quartz, Citrine, and Amethyst in an alternating circle. Next, hold a Clear Quartz over the animal's abdomen and turn clockwise for 10 minute healing sessions.

DOG – CAT AGGRESSION – Program a Blue Quartz for the dog and a Fire Agate for the cat to become energetic friends. Securely attach the crystals to the animal's collar/harness and cleanse every 30 days.

DOMINANCE – Attach a Golden Topaz and Blue Tiger's Eye to the animal's collar/harness to calm down dominance issues. Cleanse every 30 days.

DRIED BEANS – For dried bean consumption, use a Bloodstone and Emerald combination over the stomach area for a 30-minute session.

DRINKING (EXCESSIVE) – Program an Aquamarine and Onyx to calm down this excessive behavior. Securely attach the Aquamarine to the underside of the drinking container and securely attach the Onyx to the animal's collar/harness.

DROOLING (EXCESSIVE) – Twice a day work on healing the animal's throat chakra with Carnelian and Onyx in your dominant hand turning counter-clockwise movements.

DROPSY (FISH) – Program and securely attach Carnelian and Topaz to the outside of the aquarium for 14 days.

DRY COAT – Make a Turquoise and Clear Quartz gem elixir, charging for 1 hour, and generously mist the animal's coat once a day for 14 days.

DRY EYES – Use an Aquamarine gem elixir, charging for 30 minutes, and place three drops in each eye twice a day for dry eye issues.

DRY HEAVES – Surround the animal with two pieces of Pyrite and two Tiger's Eyes, alternating stones, for 15 minute intervals to help calm down this issue.

DRY SKIN – Make an Aquamarine and Clear Quartz gem elixir, charging for 1 hour, and gently mist the dry skin areas once a day.

DYSPLASIA (HIP & ELBOW) – For elbow issues, securely attach a programmed Emerald as close as you can to the area. For hip issues, securely attach a programmed Fluorite as close as you can to the area.

EAR CANAL ABLATION – Attach a Sapphire to the animal as close as you can to the ear area. Cleanse every 30 days.

EAR BLISTERS – Make a Blue Agate and Amethyst gem elixir, charging for 30 minutes, and drench a cotton-ball with the charged water. Gently pat the ear blisters three times a day with the charged water.

EAR ITCHING – When the animal is calm, hold a Topaz in your dominant hand and a Carnelian in your opposite hand and slowly work clockwise around the animal's ear area.

EAR INFECTION –Attach a programmed Amber and Onyx to the animal's collar/harness as close as you can to his/her ear that is infected.

EAR MITES – Make a Black Tourmaline and Clear Quartz gem elixir, charging for 1 hour, and very lightly mist the area of concern twice a day.

EAR PROBLEMS (GENERAL)- Attach a programmed Amber to the animal's collar/harness as close as you can to the Bud chakras for best results.

EATING DIRT – Make an Amber and Moss Agate gem elixir, charging for 2 hours, and lightly mist his/her food with the charged water. Next, generously mist any open areas of dirt outside that he/she is getting into!

EATING FECES – Make an Amber and Carnelian gem elixir, charging for 1 hour, and lightly mist his/her food with the charged water. Next, generously mist his/her mouth before being let outside or to roam where he/she can get into feces.

EATING GARBAGE – Use an Amber and Onyx gem elixir, charging for 2 hours, and lightly mist his/her food with the charged water. Next, generously mist around the area that the garbage is located, both indoors and outdoors.

EATING GRASS (EXCESSIVE) – Make an Amber and Tree Agate gem elixir, charging for 1 hour, and generously mist his/her mouth before being left alone with a grassy area.

EATING ROCKS – Use an Amber and Brown Jasper gem elixir, charging for 3 hours, and thoroughly mist all rocks that are available for the animal to get into.

EATING PROBLEMS – Securely attach a programmed Golden Topaz to the animal's collar/harness. Next, make an Aquamarine gem elixir, charging for 1 hour, and lightly mist his/her food for feeding time.

ECZEMA – Program an Ocean Jasper and securely attach this to the animal's collar/harness. Cleanse and re-program every 14 days.

EGG BINDING – Program a Smoky Quartz and Moonstone to help resolve this issue and securely attach these crystals to the underside of the bird's cage.

ELBOW CALLUSES – Make a Peridot and Ammonite gem elixir, charging for 2 hours, and generously apply the charged water to the calluses once a day.

ELBOW DAMAGE – Securely attach an Emerald and Onyx combination to the animal's collar/harness as close as you can to the area in concern.

EMOTIONAL TRAUMA – Surround the animal with alternating Jade and Howlite stones, at least two of each stone, and allow the animal to become calm and relaxed again.

ENERGY BOOST – Attach a programmed Green Amber to the animal's collar/harness when they need an energy boost!

ENTROPION SURGERY– Surround the animal with Blue Lace Agate and Fluorite, after the surgery, at least twice a day for 15-minute sessions for 7 days. After 7 days, securely attach this crystal combination to the animal's collar/harness.

EPILEPSY – Attach Black Tourmaline, Amber, and Jasper to the animal's collar/harness to work on epilepsy issues.

EXCITEMENT URINATION – Make sure to program a Rhodonite and securely attach to the animal's collar/harness. Cleanse and re-program every 30 days.

EXTERNAL PARASITES (FISH) – Attach a piece of Copper near the center and bottom of the outside of the aquarium. Cleanse every 7 days and repeat as needed.

EUTHANASIA – When faced with this issue, make sure to have Angelite and a Cross Stone with you before this begins. Place the Angelite at the crown chakra and the Cross Stone at the heart chakra of the animal before saying goodbye.

EYE (CLOUDY) – Make an Aquamarine and Emerald gem elixir, charging for 1 hour, and place 3 drops in each eye that is affected.

EYE (SWOLLEN) – Hold an Optical Calcite and Azurite in your dominant hand turn clockwise around the eye area three times a day.

EYE PROBLEMS (GENERAL) – Securely attach a programmed Topaz to the animal's collar/harness for general eye issues. You can also make a Topaz gem elixir, charging for 1 hour, and place 3 drops in each eye for general eye problems.

EYE SIGHT (POOR) – Attach a Tiger's Eye and Peridot to the animal's collar/harness to help ease issues with poor eye sight.

EYE TEARING – Make an Onyx and Aquamarine gem elixir, charging for 1 hour, and place 3 drops in the eye twice a day.

FACIAL TWITCHING – Hold a Black Phantom Quartz within 12 inches of the animal and slowly work clockwise around the physical body first and then over the head and crown chakra. Cleanse after each session.

FAINTING – Animal's that faint can need an energy stabilizer. Attach a programmed Amethyst and Lapis Lazuli to the collar/harness and cleanse every 14 days.

FEAR (GENERAL) – Attach a programmed Smoky Quartz and Rose Quartz to the animal's collar/harness for general fear issues. Cleanse regularly.

FEAR BITING – Securely attach a programmed Agate to the animal's collar/harness and cleanse every 14 days.

FEAR OF BLANKETS – Begin by making a Lime Green Calcite gem elixir, charging for 1 hour, and gently mist all of the blankets that he/she comes in contact with. Next program this crystal and securely attach to the animal's collar/harness to help ease this fear.

FEAR OF FIREWORKS – Make sure you have Aventurine and Jasper attached securely to the animal's collar/harness before the fireworks start to go off to bring down the fear and anxiety levels.

FEAR OF NIGHT/DARKNESS – Program and place a Citrine in the animal's sleeping area, such as his/her cage or crate, and securely attach a programmed Amethyst to the animal's collar/harness to ease night and darkness fears.

FEAR OF SPRAY BOTTLES – Make an Eilat Stone gem elixir and place the charged water in the spray bottle that the animal is fearful of. Place this bottle on the ground and allow the animal to come to the bottle and see that it will not hurt them. Once they have become adjusted to this, gently mist from this bottle three times a day for 7 days.

FEAR OF VACUUM CLEANER – First make a Jasper and Aquamarine gem elixir, charging for 1 hour, and place this charged water in a mist bottle. Next, attach this crystal combination to the animal's collar/harness. Before using the vacuum cleaner lightly mist the areas that will be swept and also around the area that the animal will be.

FEAR OF NOISES – Program a Smoky Quartz and Amber combination and attach securely to the animal's collar/harness. Cleanse every 30 days.

FEAR OF VET – Attach a Silver Gray Moonstone to the animal's collar/harness before taking them to the vet to calm fears of this visit.

FEATHER CYSTS (BIRD) – Make a Clear Tourmaline gem elixir, charging for 1 hour, and gently mist the areas of concern three times a day.

FEATHER PLUCKING (BIRDS) – Program and attach a Peridot to the underside of the bird's cage. Cleanse and re-program every 14 days.

FENCE BASHING – Make an Azurite gem elixir, charging for 2 hours, and thoroughly spray all of the areas that are being attacked during the fence bashing episodes. Next, attach the Azurite to the animal's collar/harness. Cleanse every 30 days.

FERTILITY ISSUES FOR BREEDING – Attach a programmed Zoisite to the female's collar/harness and a programmed Emerald to the male's collar/harness for fertility issues dealing with breeding.

FEVER – When an animal has a fever, make sure to pick up your Aqua Aura and turn this clockwise around the animal for a 15-minute session three times a day.

FIGHTING OVER TREATS – Make sure the person holds a Fire Agate in his/her hand for a few minutes before handing these goodies out to the animals. State your intention with the crystal and have a clear focus of what you want before and during this time period. The animal's energy will correspond with the crystal and your intention.

FIN ROT (FISH) – Attach an Aquamarine to the left side of the aquarium and an Onyx to the right side of the aquarium, both on the outside of the tank, to balance out and heal this issue.

FISH HOOKS – Hold a Black Tourmaline and Aqua Aura around the area that was snagged by the fishhook and turn clockwise movements over the entire area for 10 minutes.

FISH INJURIES (GENERAL) – Make sure to surround the tank/pond with alternating Turquoise and Aquamarine to help heal general fish injury issues.

FISHING LINE AGGRESSIVENESS – Make sure you have Hematite and Howlite in a combination casing attached to any fishing lines you have around. This combination will deter the animal and keep aggressiveness at bay.

FOAMING AT MOUTH (NOT RABIES) – Hold an Eilat Stone in your dominant hand and circle the entire head area of the animal, from left to right, each time making larger circling motions. Circle this direction 10 times and then reverse the direction as well as the size of the circles should decrease with each reverse movement. Lastly, hold the Eilat Stone over the animal's crown chakra and turn clockwise for 5 more minutes.

FOCUS – Attach a Tiger's Eye to the animal's collar/harness programmed for focus issues. Cleanse every 30 days.

FOOD ALLERGIES – Make a programmed Carnelian gem elixir, charging for 30 minutes, and lightly mist the food before feeding time to bring about a balanced state.

FOOD CLEANSING – Hold a Clear Quartz Terminated crystal in your dominant hand and slowly turn the crystal clockwise 3 times over each piece of food before eating to remove toxins. Cleanse after each use.

FOOT PAD – CRACKED – Use a Brown Jasper gem elixir, charging for 1 hour, and generously apply the charged water to the areas of concern.

FOOT PAD – CUT – Make a Brown Jasper and Carnelian gem elixir, charging for 20 minutes, and gently mist the cut areas of the foot pad three times a day.

FOOT PAD – INJURY – Attach securely a Brown Jasper and Rose Quartz with hypoallergenic tape as close as you can to the footpad area. Check every hour to see how the animal is responding to the energies.

FLATULENCE – For general issues, attach a Smoky Quartz to the animal's collar/harness for every day general healing. For short onset bursts, place a Smoky Quartz on each side of the animal's abdomen and hold a Golden Topaz over the animal's mid-abdominal section for 10 minutes.

FLATWORMS – Place Clear Quartz on each side of the animal's lower abdomen and hold a Ruby near the animal's root chakra. Turn the Ruby clockwise for 10 minutes. Repeat three times a day.

FLEA CONTROL – Make an Amethyst and Clear Quartz gem elixir, charging for 30 minutes, and thoroughly mist the entire animal or area of concern. Repeat every day for 7 days.

FLU – Use Rainforest Jasper to help ease the symptoms of the flu. Surround the animal with this crystal up to three times a day, or place near his/her solar plexus chakra for best results.

FLUFFED FEATHERS – Attach a White Jade to the underside of the bird's cage for dealing with excessive amounts of fluffed feathers.

FLUID AROUND THE LUNGS – Place Bloodstone on each side of the animal, and hold Amber near the lung area. Turn the Amber counter-clockwise for a 10-minute session.

FRACTURES – Securely attach Calcite and Mother of Pearl with hypoallergenic tape to the splinted area. Cleanse, re-program, and re-attach every day.

FROSTBITE – Make sure you hold Purple Fluorite and Calcite in your dominant hand and slowly circle the areas of frostbite in a counter-clockwise motion for as long as the animal will allow.

FUNGUS (FISH) – Securely attach one Clear Quartz Crystal to each side of the aquarium and one Aquamarine to the top of the tank. Cleanse and repeat every 4 days.

FURNITURE ISSUES – Make an Onyx and Emerald gem elixir, charging for 2 hours, and gently mist all furniture areas that the animal will claw, chew, bite, scratch, or climb on to deter this behavior.

GAGGING/RETCHING ISSUES – Hold Celestite around the animal's brachial chakra first and slowly move this down to the animal's throat chakra, turning clockwise during the entire session.

GALL BLADDER – Place Red Jasper on each side of the animal's lower abdomen and hold Hematite above the abdomen turning counter-clockwise for 10 minutes to help ease gall bladder issues.

GARLIC - For garlic consumption, use Iolite over the stomach area for a 30-minute session.

GASPING FOR AIR (FISH) – Make a Turquoise gem elixir, charging for 20 minutes, and place 20 drops in the aquarium for every 10 gallons of water. Next, securely attach the Turquoise to the outside of the tank.

GENERAL CLEANSING – Hold Clear Quartz, Turquoise, and Amber in your dominant hand and use large brush stroke motions within 12 inches of the animal's physical body, moving from head to paw.

GENERAL HEALING (ACHES/PAINS) – Place Epidote, Rose Quartz and Amethyst in an alternating circle around the animal. Allow the animal to rest for as long as they desire.

GIARDIA – Place Clear Quartz on each side of the animal and Golden Topaz over the animal's lower abdomen area turning counter-clockwise for 10 minutes.

GILL FLUKES (FISH) – Attach a programmed Rutilated Quartz to the top of the aquarium tank lid and cleanse every 5 days.

GIVING BIRTH – Make sure to surround the area with Emerald and Strawberry Quartz to help ease the surrounding energies of the birthing process.

GIZZARD PROBLEMS (GENERAL) – Attach Sodalite to the underside of the animal's cage and cleanse every 14 days.

GLAUCOMA – Attach a Tanzine Quartz and Clear Quartz to the animal's collar/harness. You can also make a gem elixir of these two crystals, charging for 1 hour, and place 3 drops in each affected eye twice a day.

GOUT – Allow the animal to rest with Fluorite and Jasper around its lower abdomen for as long as they desire.

GRAPES - For grape consumption, use Amber over the stomach area for a 30-minute session.

GRASS ALLERGY – Make a Rainforest Jasper gem elixir, charging for 1 hour, and gently mist all areas that come into contact with the grass. If this is a smaller animal, gently mist the entire body once a day, and securely attach the programmed Rainforest to the animal's collar/harness.

GRAZING PROBLEMS – Attach a Moss Agate and Rhodochrosite combination to the animal's collar/harness to balance out this issue.

GREEN TOMATOES/PLANT LEAVES – For green tomatoes or plant leaf consumption, use Botswana Agate over the stomach area for a 30-minute session.

GRIEVING ISSUES – Attach a programmed Poppy Jasper and Clear Quartz to the animal's collar/harness and cleanse every 7 days.

GROOMER ISSUES – Make sure the animal has a programmed Lapis Lazuli attached to his/her collar before a visit with the groomer to calm down any underlying issues.

GROWLING – Program and securely attach a Green Jade to the animal's collar/harness to help with growling issues. Cleanse and re-program every 30 days.

GUARDIAN ANGELS – Attach Angelite to the animal's collar, harness, cage, or crate to bring about a stronger connection with his/her guardian angels.

GUIDE DOGS – Program and attach a Herkimer Diamond and Angelite combination to the dog's harness to help in aiding his/her training and assistance with humans.

GUM PROBLEMS (GENERAL) – Make a Mahogany Obsidian gem elixir, charging for 1 hour, and gently rub the charged water over the gums once a day.

HAIR LOSS – Use a Snowflake Obsidian and Clear Quartz gem elixir, charging for 1 hour, and gently mist and comb the areas where hair loss is of concern. Repeat once a day.

HAIR PROBLEMS (GENERAL) – Make a Tanzanite gem elixir, charging for 2 hours, and gently mist the animal from head to paw once a day to balance out these energies.

HAIRBALLS (EXCESSIVE) – Attach Fluorite and a Herkimer Diamond securely to the animal's collar/harness to decrease the energy surrounding this issue.

HAIRLESS ANIMALS – To balance out his/her energies, have the animal wear a Tanzanite and Amethyst crystal combination on the collar/harness. Cleanse every 30 days.

HEAD AND LATERAL LINE EROSION (FISH) – Attach a Ruby to the outside of the aquarium bottom and cleanse every 7 days.

HEAD BUTTING (EXCESSIVE) – Twice a day, use Clear Fluorite and Sodalite as a general healing over the brachial chakra, crown chakra and head area.

HEAD SHAKING – Program and securely attach a Green Tourmaline to the animal's collar/harness near the head area.

HEARING ISSUES – Attach two Lapis Lazuli, one on each side of the collar/harness, for best results with hearing issues.

HEART (GENERAL ISSUES) – Securely attach a Bloodstone to the top of the harness and Hematite to the bottom of the harness to balance out this energy.

HEARTWORM – Make a Hematite and Topaz gem elixir, charging for 2 hours, and place 10 drops in the food before feeding time for 10 days.

HEAT STROKE – Hold Brazilianite in your dominant hand and slowly work over the entire physical body from head to paws and then back to the head area, turning clockwise for the entire session.

HEMLOCK – For hemlock consumption, use a Golden Calcite and Hematite combination over the stomach area for a 30-minute session.

HERNIA – Place Brown Carnelian on each side of the area of concern and hold an Orange Carnelian in your dominant hand for this healing session. Allow the session to last as long as the animal desires.

HIBERNATION (REPTILES) – Place one Red Jasper and one Clear Quartz in opposite sides of the tank to boost hibernation energy issues

HICCUPS – Hold an Amethyst in your dominant hand and Lapis Lazuli in your opposite hand. Turn the crystals clockwise and opposite each other around the animal for a 10-minute session to subside hiccup concerns. You can also make a gem elixir of the above crystals, charging for 10 minutes, and place 10 drops on the animal's tongue.

HIDING BEHAVIOR – Make a Pink Topaz and Jade gem elixir, charging for 1 hour, and thoroughly mist all of the animals hiding places. Next, attach these programmed crystals to the animal's collar/harness.

HIGH STRUNG ANIMALS – Attach a programmed Lapis Lazuli to the animal's collar/harness to calm down his/her high-strung energy.

HIND LEG WEAKNESS – Attach Hematite as close as you can to his/her hind leg and cleanse every day. You can also place one Hematite on each side of the hind leg and allow the animal is rest and the Hematite to draw out the issues causing the weakness.

HIP PROBLEMS – Securely attach Petrified Wood to the animal's harness near the hip area for best results.

HISSING (EXCESSIVE) – Make a Golden Citrine and Tiger's Eye gem elixir, charging for 1 hour, and place 5 drops of the charge water on the animal's tongue or 10 drops in the water container. You can also program and attach these crystals to the animal's collar/harness.

HISTOPLASMOSIS – Hold Fluorite and Calcite in your dominant hand and slowly turn them counter-clockwise around the animal for a 10-minute crystal session three times a day.

HIVES – Surround the animal with Clear Quartz crystals, all pointing in a clockwise manner, and hold an Amber piece over one of the hives. Turn the Amber piece in a counter-clockwise motion three times and move to the next hive area until they have all been worked. Repeat as needed.

HOME ALONE ISSUES – Program Cobaltite and place near the doorway when you leave. When you return home, remove the Cobaltite and cleanse. Make sure this is out of reach for the animal at home.

HOOKWORMS – Place Clear Quartz on each side of the animal's lower abdominal area and hold a Citrine near the animal's sacral chakra. Turn the Citrine clockwise for 10 minutes. Repeat three times a day.

HOPS – For hops consumption, use a Turquoise and Bloodstone combination over the stomach area for a 30-minute session.

HORMONE ISSUES (GENERAL) – Securely attach a programmed Green Fluorite to the animal's collar/harness. For best results, cleanse every 14 days.

HORSE FLIES – Make a Citrine gem elixir, charging for 1 hour, and generously mist all areas of concern.

HORSE HOOF ISSUES – Use a Brown Carnelian in a general healing session, working around all four hooves in a clockwise motion. You can also make a gem elixir, charging for 30 minutes, and gently mist the areas of concern for an extra healing boost.

HORSESHOES – Jasper works best for a general crystal healing for horseshoes. Work clockwise around the horse for this session and repeat as needed.

HOUSETRAINING – For this two-step process you will need a Hematite, Rose Quartz and Smoky Quartz. First, make a Hematite gem elixir, charging for 1 hour, and gently mist all of the areas that the animal is not supposed to be going to, but already has. Next, program a Rose Quartz and Smoky Quartz, and attach them to the animal's collar/harness and lovingly show the animal where you want them to go.

HOWLING (DOGS - EXCESSIVE) – Program and attach Amethyst and Sodalite to the animal's collar/harness to help calm this behavioral issue.

HUMPING BEHAVIOR – Program and attach a Smoky Quartz to the animal's collar/harness that is expressing this behavioral issue.

HUNTING AGGRESSION (INCREASE) – Program and attach Apache Tears to the animal's collar/harness to increase his/her hunting aggression.

HUNTING AGGRESSION (PREVENT) – Program and attach Sugilite and Rose Quartz to the animal's collar/harness to decrease his/her hunting aggression.

HERDING ISSUES (INCREASE) – To increase the animal's natural tendency for herding, attach programmed Mochi Balls to his/her collar.

HERDING ISSUES (PREVENT) - To decrease the animal's natural tendency for herding, attach programmed Black Tourmaline and Rose Quartz to his/her collar.

HYPERACTIVITY – Securely attach Apatite to the animal's collar/harness to calm down hyperactivity issues.

ICE MELTING CHEMICALS – For ingestion of ice melting chemicals, use a Bloodstone and Verdite combination over the stomach area for a 30-minute session. If this is an irritant for the animal's paws, use this combination in a gem elixir, charging for 20 minutes and gently rinse his/her paws in this charged water.

IMMUNE SYSTEM – To give the animal's immune system a boost, place Amber in a secure copper encasement on the collar/harness area.

INABILITY TO PERCH – Program and attach Jasper and Clear Quartz to the underside of the bird's cage to help with perching ability.

INCOMPATIBLE SPECIES (FISH) – Program and attach Aventurine on each side of the aquarium tank. Cleanse and re-program every 14 days or until the fish start showing a more responsive behavioral pattern

INCONTINENCE – Attach Scapolite to the animal's collar/harness to help with this issue.

INFLAMMATION – Hold Blue Lace Agate around the areas of inflammation and turn in a clockwise motion to draw out concerns causing this issue.

INSECT STING – Make an Emerald and Moonstone gem elixir, charging for 1 hour, and gently mist or pat all of the areas that have an insect sting. Allow to air dry and repeat as needed.

INTRODUCING NEW PETS – Make sure the area is surrounded with programmed Citrine when introducing new pets to balance out the energy that is given off by each animal.

IRRITABLE BOWL – Place Halite on either side of the hip area and hold Hematite over the lower abdominal area for 15 minutes at a time.

JAUNDICE – Surround the animal with a circle of alternating Aquamarine, Carnelian, Citrine and Emerald for 15 minutes at a time.

JEALOUSY – Attach a programmed Rose Quartz and Jade to the animal's collar/harness to ease the green-eyed monster.

JUMPING FENCES – Make a Tree Agate and Brown Carnelian gem elixir, charging for 1 hour, and thoroughly mist all fences that the animal is jumping over.

JUMPING ISSUES (GENERAL) – Program and attach Angelite to the animal's collar/harness to control general jumping issues.

JUMPING ON PEOPLE – Attach a programmed Strawberry Quartz to the animal's collar/harness to control his/her tendency to jump on people.

KENNEL COUGH – Hold an Eilat Stone in your dominant hand and a Clear Quartz in your opposite hand and slowly turn them both counter-clockwise around the animal for a 10 minute session. Repeat three times a day.

KICKING PROBLEM (HORSE) – Attach a three-crystal combination of Jasper, Rose Quartz and Emerald to the horse's reins to help prevent kicking issues.

KIDNEY PROBLEMS (GENERAL) – Place Fluorite on each side of the animal and allow him/her to enjoy the vibrational healing energy for as long as he/she desires.

KNEADING (EXCESSIVE) – Attach Howlite and Clear Quartz to the animal's collar to help calm this excessive behavior.

KNEE PROBLEMS (GENERAL) – Perform a general crystal healing session around the knee area as often as needed with Ammonite. Make sure to use a clockwise motion for this session for approximately 10 minutes. You can also attach a programmed Ammonite to the animal's collar/harness if desired.

LABORED BREATHING – Hold Morganite and Rose Quartz in opposite hands and slowly work in counter-clockwise motions around the animal's chest area.

LACTATION – Attach a Desert Rose to the animal's collar/harness to help with lactation issues.

LAMENESS – Attach a Coral and Hematite combination to the animal's collar/harness to help balance out this issue.

LAW ENFORCEMENT DOGS – Program and attach Leopardskin Jasper to the dog's harness to help in aiding his/her training and assistance with humans.

LEG PROBLEMS (GENERAL) – Perform a general healing session with Ammonite and Hematite working in counter-clockwise motions for 10 minute time periods.

LETHARGIC – Attach a programmed Orange Drusy Quartz to the animal's collar/harness to counteract this issue.

LICE – Make a Black Tourmaline and Amber gem elixir, charging for 1 hour, and generously spray all areas concerning this issue.

LICKING - GENERAL (EXCESSIVE) – Program and attach a Blue Topaz to the animal's collar/harness to control excessive licking.

LICKING HOUSEHOLD SURFACES – Make an Amethyst and Rose Quartz gem elixir, charging for 30 minutes, and gently mist all surfaces that the animal has been licking.

LIGAMENT PROBLEMS (GENERAL) – Hold an Opal and Black Obsidian in opposite hands and use clockwise movements throughout the entire healing session for minimum of 10 minutes. Repeat as needed.

LIGHT SENSITIVITY – Attach a programmed Rhodonite to the animal's collar/harness to help with light sensitivity issues.

LILY PLANTS – For lily plant consumption, use Kambaba Jasper over the stomach area for a 30-minute session.

LIMPING – Place Blue Lace Agates on opposite sides of the leg and hold an Ammonite in your dominant hand. Turn this clockwise to help draw out any negative energy issues. Repeat as needed.

LITTER BOX TRAINING –For two-step process you will need Smoky Quartz and Carnelian. Make a gem elixir of both crystals, charging for 1 hour, and gently mist all of the areas that the animal is not supposed to be going to, but already has. Next, program the crystals and place them on opposite sides of the litter box to encourage your animal to respond to this area.

LIVER PROBLEMS (GENERAL) – Place Iolite on each side of the animal and allow him/her to enjoy the vibrational healing energy for as long as he/she desires.

LONELINESS – Program and attach Jasper and Snowflake Obsidian to the animal's collar/harness to ease loneliness issues.

LONGEVITY – Program multiple Jade stones for this issue. Attach one to the animal's collar/harness, place one in his/her sleeping area, and anywhere else he/she spends a great deal of time. Remember to cleanse and re-program them every 30 days.

LOST ANIMALS – Program an Aventurine with the intention of finding the lost animal. Next, place this over a picture of the animal and keep this close to the front door to help the animal find a safe return home. To help keep an animal from becoming lost, make sure you program an Aventurine and attach this to the animal's collar/harness.

LOOSE STOOLS – Surround the animal with Red Jasper and hold Rhodochrosite over the lower abdominal area for a 10-minute time period.

LOOSE TEETH – To help with loose teeth, make a Fluorite gem elixir, charging for 1 hour, and gently rub the animal's gum line with the charged water three times a day.

LUNG PROBLEMS (GENERAL) – Hold Morganite in your dominant hand and slowly turn this clockwise over the chest area for 15 minutes or as along as the animal will allow.

LYME DISEASE – Attach Black Coral and Ruby to the animal's collar/harness to help balance out this issue.

LYMPH NODES – Perform a crystal healing session with Smithsonite, turning counter-clockwise, around the area for as long as the animal will allow.

MACADAMIA NUTS - For macadamia nut consumption, use Charoite over the stomach area for a 30-minute session.

MAGGOTS (PREVENTION OF) – Make a Hematite and Apache Tears gem elixir, charging for 1 hour, and generously mist all areas of concern.

MANE ISSUES (GENERAL) – Use a Mica elixir, charging for 1 hour, and lightly mist and brush all areas of concern.

MARKING TERRITORY – Make a Pearl and Onyx gem elixir, charging for 1 hour, and generously mist all areas that the animal is marking. Next, securely attach this combination of crystals to his/her collar or harness. Repeat every 14 days until issue has subsided.

MASSAGE – Use a flat Clear Quartz while working with animal massage sessions. If you wish to incorporate a healing and massage session together, use the appropriate crystal for the ailment being treated.

MASTITIS – Use Chiastolite, Moonstone, and Turquoise in a crystal healing session, turning them clockwise one at a time around the area of concern. After each crystal has had its own time to work, hold all three in your dominant hand and work one large clockwise motion around the entire animal.

MEDICATION – When giving medication to your animal, make sure to cleanse this of any toxins before administering. Hold a Clear Quartz Terminated crystal in your dominant hand and slowly turn the crystal clockwise 3 times over the medicine before giving this to the animal. Cleanse after each use.

MEOWING (EXCESSIVE) – Attach a programmed Snow Quartz to the cat's collar to calm down this excessive behavior.

MISTLETOE PLANTS – For mistletoe plant consumption, use a Citrine and Hematite combination over the stomach area for a 30-minute session.

MITES – Make a Black Obsidian and Sodalite gem elixir, charging for 2 hours, and thoroughly mist all areas of concern.

MORNING GLORY – For morning glory consumption, use a Fluorite and Turquoise combination over the stomach area for a 20-minute session.

MOTION SICKNESS – Attach a programmed Aquamarine to the animal's collar/harness before traveling to avoid motion sickness issues.

MOLDY FOODS – For moldy food consumption, use Ocean Jasper over the stomach area for a 15-minute session.

MOULTING (EXCESSIVE) – Attach a programmed Tanzanite securely to the underside of the bird's cage to balance out these excessive energies.

MOUNTING BEHAVIOR – Program and attach a Moonstone and Amethyst combination to the animal's collar/harness to help with this behavioral issue.

MOUTH PROBLEMS (GENERAL) – Make an Aquamarine and Clear Quartz gem elixir, charging for 1 hour, and place 5 drops in the animal's mouth or 10 drops in the water container.

MUCUS PROBLEMS – Hold an Aqua Aura and Topaz near the head and nose area and turn in a clockwise motion 5 times to draw out the stagnant energies. Next, cleanse the crystals thoroughly before making a gem elixir, charging for 1 hour. Place 5 drops of the charged water on the animal's tongue twice a day.

MULCH – For mulch consumption, use Picasso Jasper over the stomach area for a 30-minute session.

MUSCLE SPASMS – Make an Amazonite gem elixir, charging for 30 minutes, and lightly mist the affected muscles twice a day. For a direct resolution, place this crystal within 2 inches of the affected area and turn clockwise to draw out the negative energies.

MUSCULAR SYSTEM – Hold Mochi Balls in your dominant hand and work counter-clockwise around the animal and his/her aura field. Allow the session to last as long as they will permit.

MUSHROOMS – For mushroom consumption, use an Emerald and Citrine combination over the stomach area for a 30-minute session.

Practical Crystal Healing

MUSTARD SEEDS – For mustard seed consumption, use a Garnet and Black Tourmaline combination over the stomach area for a 20-minute session.

MUZZLE TRAINING – Program and secure an Apatite to the outside of the muzzle for a calm and relaxed approach to this type of training.

NAIL LOSS – Hold Onyx and Brown Carnelian in your dominant hand and the animal's paw in your opposite hand. Slowly work around the entire area, circling the animal's paw. Place the animal's paw down and slowly move the crystals over the nail areas one at a time. Cleanse after a complete session.

NAIL SPLIT – Make a Blackstar and Brown Jasper gem elixir, charging for 1 hour, and gently mist all areas of concern.

NAIL TRIM BLEEDING – Use a Bloodstone and Onyx gem elixir, charging for 20 minutes, and drench a cotton-ball with the charged water. Apply a bit of pressure to the nail with the drenched cotton-ball to help stop the bleeding and heal quickly.

NAIL PROBLEMS (GENERAL) – When the animal is resting, place Jasper at each of the paws that are of concern and all the energies to heal for as long as the animal permits.

NASAL DRIP – Hold a Smithsonite and Clear Quartz in your dominant hand and turn them clockwise around the head and nose area for 10 minutes to help balance the energy from this issue.

NASAL IRRITATION – Program a Blue Fluorite and slowly move this crystal in a forward motion, starting at the bridge between the animal's eye and working towards the end of his/her nose. Repeat the same movement as many times as the animal will allow to absorb this healing energy.

NEGATIVE ENERGIES – Securely attach Amber to the animal's collar, harness, cage, or crate to cleanse the animal and area of negative energies.

NERVOUSNESS – Program and attach Amazonite and Snow Quartz to the animal's collar/harness to calm down nervousness tension.

NERVOUS SYSTEM –Hold Nephrite in your dominant hand and work counter-clockwise around the animal and his/her aura field. Allow the session to last as long as they will permit.

NEUTERING – Make sure to program and attach Aventurine to the animal's collar/harness before the surgery and cleanse and re-attach after the surgery.

NEW BABY IN THE HOUSE – Program and attach Jasper and Stichtite to the animal before the new baby comes home for the first time. Remove and cleanse every 30 days.

NOSE BLEEDS – Hold Bloodstone along the bridge of the animal's nose and move in a backward motion from the tip to the eyes to help stop a nosebleed.

NOSE PROBLEMS (GENERAL) –Hold Larimar in your dominant hand and turn this clockwise around the head and nose area for 10 minutes to help balance out this energy.

NURSING – Program and attach Moonstone and Desert Rose to the general area where the mother is nursing. Make sure to keep out of reach from the mother and the babies.

OBEDIENCE – Program Cerussite and attach to the animal's collar/harness to help with obedience issues.

OBESITY – Program and attach Moonstone and Rose Quartz to the animal's collar/harness for a long-term result.

OBSESSIVENESS –Program Celestite for obsessiveness issues and attach to the animal's collar/harness. Make sure to cleanse regularly.

OILY SKIN – Make a Hematite and Clear Quartz gem elixir, charging for 1 hour, and gently rub down oily skin areas. Allow the skin to air dry.

ONIONS/ONION POWDER – For onion consumption, use a Jade and Citrine combination over the stomach area for a 30-minute session.

OUTSIDE DOG HOUSE – Program and attach a Hawk's Eye to the doghouse to provide an energetic safe haven. Cleanse and repeat every 30-day.

OVER-EATING - Charge and cleanse food with Amber and Turquoise by turning these in a counter-clockwise motion to help prevent over-eating issues.

OVER-HEATING –Hold Botswana Agate in your dominant hand and slowly work over the entire physical body from head to paws and then back to the head area, turning clockwise in motion the entire session.

OVER-STIMULATION – Over-stimulation can be resolved by attaching Malachite securely to the animal's collar/harness before, during, and after the stimulation time period.

PACK BEHAVIOR – To increase a pack like behavior in animals, make sure they are all wearing programmed Chrysoprase attached to his/her collar or harness.

PACK LEADER – Program and securely attach Malachite and Azurite to the animal's collar that needs to establish a pack leader role.

PAIN (GENERAL) – Place a Clear Quartz, Turquoise, and Emerald near the affected area for 5 minutes. Slowly turn the crystals clockwise for 2 minutes, or as long as the animal will allow.

PANCREATITIS – Attach a programmed Ruby Zoisite to the animal's collar/harness to help with issues of pancreatitis. Cleanse every 14 days.

PANOSTEITIS – Place Fluorite and Rhodonite around the animal in an alternating crystal circle three times a day.

PANTING (EXCESSIVE) – Program and attach Unakite to the animal's collar/harness to help balance this energy issue.

PARALYSIS – Attach Amazonite and Peridot near the area of paralysis, or as close as possible. Once a day provide the animal with a Clear Quartz crystal point general healing over his/her entire physical body.

PARVO – Make a Green Jasper, Moonstone, and Pyrite gem elixir, charging for 1 hour, and place 5 drops on the animal's tongue three times a day.

PATIENCE – Program and attach Howlite to the animal's collar to bring about more patience in his/her energy fields.

PAW PROBLEMS (GENERAL) – Using hypoallergenic tape, secure Blackstar to the paw that is of concern. Allow the animal to wear this for one day and remove in the evening before sleeping. Repeat as needed.

PET SITTER – Make sure to have two Blue Quartz for this issue. Program one for the animal to have attached to his/her collar or harness and the second one should be made available for the pet sitter to carry when he/she is visiting the animal.

PESTICIDES/FERTILIZER ISSUES – For pesticide and fertilizer issues, use a Malachite and Hematite combination over the stomach area for a 30-minute session. If this is an irritant for the animal's paws, use this combination in a gem elixir, charging for 30 minutes and gently rinse his/her paws in this charged water.

PICKY EATER – Use a Clear Quartz and Carnelian to charge the animal's food and remove toxins before eating.

PINWORMS (HORSES) –Place one Black Tourmaline on each side of the animal's lower abdominal area and hold a Golden Topaz near the animal's abdomen. Turn the Golden Topaz clockwise for 10 minutes. Repeat twice a day.

PLANT ALLERGY – Make a Pink Tourmaline and Moss Agate gem elixir, charging for 1 hour, and gently mist all areas of the plants that the animal comes into contact with. You can also mist the entire animal once a day, and securely attach the programmed crystals to the animal's collar/harness.

PLAQUE BUILDUP – Use an Onyx and Amber gem elixir, charging for 30 minutes, and gently rub the charged water over the animal's teeth and gums. If he/she will not allow you to do this, place 10 drops in his/her water container.

PLAYFUL BEHAVIOR – To bring about a more playful behavior, attach a programmed Orange Calcite to the animal's collar/harness.

PLAYING WITH PREY – Program and attach a Black Obsidian and Peridot to the animal's collar/harness to tone down this aggressive play. Make sure to cleanse every 14 days.

PLUGGED NOSTRILS – Program Blue Fluorite and Clear Quartz for this issue and slowly move these crystals in a forward motion, starting at the bridge between the animal's eye and working toward the end of his/her nose. Repeat the same movement as many times as the animal will allow to absorb this healing energy.

PNEUMONIA – Place one piece of Fluorite on each side of the animal's chest and hold one above the chest circling in a clockwise motion for 10 minutes.

POINSETTIA PLANTS – For poinsettia plant consumption, use a White Jade and Emerald combination over the stomach area for a 20-minute session.

POISON (RECOVERING FROM) – Place Diamond, Peridot, and Sunstone around the animal in an alternating crystal circle. Allow the animal to remain as long as they desire and repeat three times a day.

POISON IVY – For poison ivy consumption, use a Brown Jasper and Turquoise combination over the stomach area for a 30-minute session. If the animal is breaking out in a poison ivy rash, make a gem elixir from the same crystals, charging for 30 minutes, and gently mist the areas that are infected.

POND ISSUES (GENERAL) – Place Clear Quartz, Moldavite, and Aquamarine in an alternating crystal circle around the pond to balance out these energies.

POTATO LEAVES/STEMS - For potato leaves or stem consumption, use Lodestone over the stomach area for a 20-minute session.

POUNCING – Program and securely attach Rose Quartz and Sugilite to the animal's collar/harness to calm down this behavioral pattern.

PREDATORY BEHAVIOR – To calm down predatory behavior, attach a programmed Chalcedony and Pearl to the animal's collar. Cleanse every 30 days.

PREGNANCY – For pregnancy concerns make sure the mother is surrounded by Carnelian, Emerald, Turquoise, and Amber. If you cannot surround her with these crystals, make sure to attach them to her collar/harness to provide a balanced energy during the pregnancy.

PREMATURE BABIES – Surround any premature babies with alternating crystals of Ruby and Sapphire to balance out the energies to help them grow and survive.

PROTECTION (ANIMAL) – Program and securely attach Angelite to the animal's collar/harness for protection energies.

PROTECTION (CAGE/CRATE) – Make sure to place Amber and Black Tourmaline in opposite corners of the cage/crate to provide a balanced protective state.

PULLING OUT FUR – Make a Pecos Diamonds gem elixir, charging for 30 minutes, and gently mist the animal from head to paw. Next, circle the animal in a clockwise manner with a programmed Clear Quartz five times or as long as the animal will allow.

PULLING ON LEASH – Program two Amethyst crystals, one to be attached to the animal's collar/harness and the second one for the person to have in his/her hand or pocket when walking.

PUPPY NIPPING - Make a Smoky Quartz gem elixir, charging for 2 hours, and gently mist the puppy's mouth area every time he/she tries to nip.

PURRING (EXCESSIVE) –Attach a programmed Blue Lace Agate to the cat's collar/harness to calm down this excessive behavior.

PYOMETRA – Place Ruby, Sodalite, and Turquoise in an alternating crystal circle surrounding the lower abdominal area of the female. Allow the animal to relax and enjoy the vibrational healing for as long as she desires.

QUARANTINED FISH – Program and attach an Onyx and Turquoise to the outside of the aquarium, one on each side, to balance out this energy.

QUIVERING TAIL – Attach a combination of Peridot, Rose Quartz, and Turquoise to the animal's collar/harness to calm down this behavioral issue.

RABIES – Make a Hematite, Clear Quartz, and Turquoise gem elixir, charging for 1 hour, and place 20 drops in the animal's water container.

RAGE SYNDROME – Program and attach Garnet and Peridot to the animal's collar/harness for best results.

RAISINS - For raisin consumption, use Nephrite over the stomach area for a 30-minute session.

RASHES – Make a Rhyolite gem elixir, charging for 1 hour, and lightly mist all of the area covered in a rash.

REARING – Attach a programmed Hematite to the reins before riding. After each session remove and cleanse.

RED MANGE – Use a Blue Quartz gem elixir, charging for 2 hours, and lightly mist all areas of concern.

RED MITES – Use a Black Obsidian and Fluorite gem elixir, charging for 1 hour, and thoroughly mist all areas of concern.

REFUSING COMMANDS – Attach a Flint and Amber combination to the animal's collar/harness to help with command issues.

REGURGITATION – Attach a Sodalite and Clear Quartz to the underside of the bird's cage for best results.

RELOCATION – Surround the animal with Amethyst and Rose Quartz for balancing out these new energies. He/she can also wear this crystal combination attached to the top of his/her collar or harness.

REPRODUCTIVE SYSTEM – Attach Garnet and Moonstone to the animal's collar/harness for best results when working with reproductive issues.

RESCUED ANIMALS – Surround the animal with Angelite and Citrine to calm and ease his/her energies to be able to access the situation better.

RESCUE DOGS – Program and attach White Jade to the animal's collar/harness to help in aiding his/her training and assistance with humans.

RESPECT ISSUES – HUMANS – Make sure you have two Yellow Jade crystals for this issue. Program them both and attach one to the animal's collar/harness and have the person that is being disrespected carry the other one.

RESPECT ISSUES – OTHER ANIMALS - Make sure you have enough Blue Jade crystals for as many animal's that are involved in this situation. Program all of them and securely attach an individual crystal to each animal's collar/harness.

RESTLESSNESS BEHAVIOR – Program Lapis Lazuli and attach to the animal's collar/harness to calm restlessness behavior.

REVERSE SNEEZING – Hold Sodalite near the bridge of the animals nose and turn counter-clockwise to help remove any stagnant energy.

RHUBARB LEAVES – For rhubarb leaf consumption, use a Peridot and Black Tourmaline combination over the stomach area for a 30-minute session.

RICKETS – Make sure to place three Malachite equally distant surrounding the animal. Allow the animal to rest and absorb the vibrational work for as long as he/she desires.

RINGWORM – Place Clear Quartz on each side of the animal's lower abdomen and hold a Lapis Lazuli near the animal's abdomen. Turn the Lapis Lazuli clockwise for 10 minutes. Repeat twice a day.

ROAMING ANIMALS – For roaming animals that frequent your area, make sure you have an Infinite gem elixir already made. Charge the water for 1 hour beforehand, and store this for up to 7 days. When the animal comes around gently mist the area around your home as close as you can without scaring the animal.

ROLLING IN SMELLY THINGS – Make a Tangerine Quartz gem elixir, charging for 2 hours, and generously mist the entire animal's body. Repeat once a day until the energy is balanced.

ROUNDWORMS –Place Black Obsidian on each side of the animal's lower abdomen and hold an Iolite near the animal's abdomen. Turn the Iolite clockwise for 10 minutes. Repeat twice a day.

RUBBING AGAINST LEGS (CATS-EXCESSIVE) – Program and attach Spinel to the cat's collar to calm down this excessive behavior.

RUNNING AWAY – Have two Turquoise available for this issue. Program them both to be attracted to each other. Secure one to the animal's collar/harness and place the other one in the center part of your home.

RUNNY NOSE – Hold a Blue Topaz and Golden Topaz in your dominant hand and turn them clockwise around the head and nose area for 10 minutes to help balance the energy from this issue.

SALT – For salt consumption, use a Rhodochrosite and Malachite combination over the stomach area for a 30-minute session.

SALIVATION ISSUES – Make a Sodalite and Aquamarine gem elixir, charging for 1 hour, and place 5 drops on the animal's tongue to help with this issue.

SALMONELLA –For salmonella issues, use an Emerald and Turquoise combination over the stomach area for a 30-minute session.

SARCOPTIC MANGE – Make a Blue Opal gem elixir, charging for 1 hour, and thoroughly mist all areas that are of concern with this issue.

SCABS - Make a gem elixir with Carnelian and Cobalite, charging for 2 hours, and gently pat or mist the area that is affected.

SCOOTING – Place Garnet and Black Obsidian around the tail end of the animal and turn clockwise to draw out any stagnant energy.

SCRATCHING (EXCESSIVE) – Use an Emerald and Agate for a basic healing around the affected area. Make sure to turn the crystals clockwise to draw out any stagnant energy.

SCRATCHING AT GLASS WINDOW/DOOR – Make a Moss Agate gem elixir, charging for 2 hours, and lightly mist all areas that are being scratched. Allow this to air dry and repeat if necessary.

SCRATCHING POSTS – Make a Clear Quartz gem elixir, charging for 1 hour, and mist all areas of the scratching post.

SCREECHING (BIRDS) – Program and attach an Amethyst to the underside of the bird's cage to calm down this excessive energy.

SEIZURE – Hold a Herkimer Diamond and Iolite near the animal's brachial and crown chakras during a seizure to help soothe and calm this issue.

SELF-GROOMING (EXCESSIVE) - Securely attach a Sunstone to the animal's collar/harness to help with excessive self-grooming issues.

SELF-HEALING – To increase self-healing energies, attach Amber to his/her collar or harness and cleanse once a week.

SENIOR ANIMALS – Attach Moonstone and Angelite to the senior animal companions to allow these soothing energies to help integrate with his/her own physical body.

SEPARATION ANXIETY ISSUES – Program and attach Rhodochrosite to the animal's collar/harness before a separation issue arises so the energy can begin to work on its own and be integrated fully. Allow up to 7 days to see results. Cleanse and program every 30 days.

SHAKING – Program and securely attach Green Jade and Strawberry Quartz to the animal's collar/harness to calm this vibrational frequency.

SHEDDING (EXCESSIVE) – Make a Lodestone gem elixir, charging for 1 hour, and gently mist the animal's coat. Brush lightly and repeat twice a day to help with shedding issues.

SHELL DISEASE (REPTILES) – Make a Petalite, Obsidian, and Turquoise gem elixir, charging for 2 hours, and lightly mist the reptile first. Next, place 5 drops of this charged water in the water container. Last, place these crystals in a triangle pattern within the cage to help heal this issue on a consistent basis.

SHYNESS – Program and attach Lepidolite to the animal's collar/harness to balance out shyness issues.

SIBLING RIVALRY – Program and attach one Tektite to each sibling animal to balance out rivalry energy.

SINUS PROBLEMS (GENERAL) –Hold Eilat Stone in your dominant hand and turn this clockwise around the head and nose area for 10 minutes to help balance this energy.

SKELETAL ISSUES –Hold Blue Coral in your dominant hand and work counter-clockwise around the animal and his/her aura field. Allow the session to last as long as they will permit.

SKIN (ALLERGIES) – Make a Carnelian gem elixir, charging for 1 hour, and gently mist all areas of the skin that are having this issue.

SKIN (HEALTHY) Make a Pyrite gem elixir, and mist or rinse the skin to keep this in a healthy and balanced state.

SKIN (ODOR) – Use a Sapphire gem elixir, charging for 1 hour, and gently mist all areas of the skin that are having this issue.

SKIN WORMS (REPTILES) – Use Carnelian and Apache Tears gem elixir, and gently mist all of the areas of concern.

SLEDDING ISSUES – Program and attach Tangerine Quartz to the animal's collar/harness before sledding to allow time for the vibrational frequency to heal this concern.

SLEEPINESS (EXCESSIVE) – Place Jet in the areas that the animal is sleeping the most in. If this happens in multiple areas, either place multiple pieces of Jet, or make a gem elixir, charging for 30 minutes, and lightly mist all areas of concern.

SLEEPING IN BED – Program Rhodonite to keep the animal out of the bed and place this in the four corners of the bed frame.

SLIPPED WING – Attach Apatite to the underside of the bird's cage to help ease this issue.

SLOUGHING (REPTILES) – Place a programmed Onyx and Clear Quartz in opposite sides of the cage to balance these energies.

SNAKEBITE – Make a Green Jasper gem elixir ahead of time if the area is prone to snakebites. Charge the water for 1 hour and store in a safe container for 7 days. Rinse the snakebite generously with the charged water, then hold Hematite above the snakebite, and turn counter-clockwise to draw out all of the negative energy.

SNEEZING/SNIFFING (EXCESSIVE) –Hold Sodalite and Clear Quartz near the bridge of the animals nose and turn counter-clockwise to help remove any stagnant energy.

SNORING – Place Lapis Lazuli and Clear Quartz in opposite ends of the cage or crate to balance out energies from snoring issues.

SOCIALIZATION – Program and securely attach Garnet to the animal's collar/harness to stabilize socialization issues.

SORES (GENERAL) – Place Carnelian within 2 inches of the sore and turn first clockwise and then counter clockwise, alternating back and forth between the two. Remember to cleanse thoroughly afterwards.

SPAYED –Make sure to program and attach Moonstone to the animal's collar/harness before the surgery and cleanse and re-attach after the surgery.

SPIDER BITE –Make Brown Jasper gem elixir ahead of time if the area is prone to spider bites. Charge the water for 1 hour and store in a safe container for 7 days. Rinse the spider bite generously with the charged water, then hold Apache Tears above the spider bite, and turn counter-clockwise to draw out all of the negative energy.

SPITEFUL URINATION –Make sure to program a Green Phantom Quartz and securely attach to the animal's collar/harness. Cleanse and re-program every 30 days.

SPLEEN PROBLEMS (GENERAL) – Place Ruby Zoisite, Peridot, and Carnelian in an alternating crystal circle around the animal and allow him/her to enjoy the vibrational healing energy for as long as he/she desires.

SPLINTS – Attach Jet to the splint area or to the animal's collar/harness to help balance out these energies.

SPOOKED (HORSES) – Program and attach Snowflake Obsidian and Garnet to the horse's reins and allow the energies to integrate for 5 days.

STAGGERING – Place Purple Fluorite on opposite sides of the animal and allow them to enjoy the vibrational healing to balance this issue.

STEALING PEOPLE FOOD – Program and attach Black Tourmaline and Garnet to the animal's collar/harness. Cleanse every 14 days.

STOMACH BLOATING – Place an Amethyst at the animal's crown chakra and a Hawk's Eye over the stomach area for a deep healing.

STOMACH BLOCKAGE – Place Goldstone on each side of the animal's stomach and hold Hematite over the stomach area turning clockwise to remove any blockages.

STOMACH PROBLEMS (GENERAL) – Surround the animal with an alternating circle of Clear Quartz and Agate. Allow the animal to rest as long as they desire. Repeat as often as needed.

STRAY ANIMALS – Perform a general crystal healing session with a Rose Quartz on stray animals. Work with the energy slowly as they are strays and are coming to you for a reason.

STRESS – Program and attach Tiger's Eye and Amethyst to the animal's collar/harness to bring down his/her stress levels.

STUCK IN TREES (CATS) – For those cats who like to climb and get stuck in trees, program and securely attach Leopardskin Jasper to his/her collar. Allow his/her own energy to bring them back down next time.

SUBMISSIVE URINATION – Make sure to program a Blue Jade and securely attach to the animal's collar/harness. Cleanse and re-program every 30 days.

SUCKLING BEHAVIOR – Program and attach Celestite and Tiger's Eye to the animal's collar/harness to reduce this excessive behavior.

SUCKLING WOOL/CLOTHING – Make a Blue Opal gem elixir, charging for 30 minutes, and gently mist all items that the animal is suckling. Repeat twice a day over 5 days.

SUNBURN – Use a Peridot, Falcon's Eye, and Hematite gem elixir, charging for 1 hour, and lightly mist all sunburn areas.

SURGERY (GENERAL) – Make sure to program and attach Turquoise and Hematite to the animal's collar/harness before the surgery and cleanse and re-attach after the surgery.

SWELLING – Hold an Andean Opal near the swollen area and turn counter-clockwise to help draw out the stagnant energy.

SWIM BLADDER DISORDER (FISH) – Attach a Tiger's Eye to opposite sides of the aquarium and a Smoky Quartz to the top of the aquarium lid to help with this issue.

TAIL INJURIES – Hold Jasper in your dominant hand and gently hold the tail in the opposite hand. Slowly work the crystal in a circular motion around the tail for as long as the animal will allow.

TAIL PUMPING – Hold Unakite near the animal's abdomen and turn in a clockwise motion to ease this issue.

TAPEWORMS –Place one Fluorite on each side of the animal's lower abdomen and hold a Garnet near the animal's root chakra. Turn the Garnet clockwise for 10 minutes. Repeat three times a day.

TEA – For tea consumption, use a Ruby and Clear Quartz combination over the stomach area for a 20-minute session.

TEETH PROBLEMS (GENERAL) – Make an Apatite gem elixir, charging for 1 hour, and place 5 drops in the animal's mouth, or rub the charged water on his/her teeth and gums three times a day.

TEETH REMOVAL – After having teeth removed, surround the animal with an alternating circle of Amethyst, Dolomite, and Aquamarine. Allow the animal to remain in the circle for as long as he/she desires.

TERRITORIAL BEHAVIOR – Program and attach Moonstone to the animal's collar/harness to ease territorial behavior.

TETHERING ISSUES – Attach a Rose Quartz and Smoky Quartz to the animal's collar/harness to help calm these issues and concerns.

THERAPY DOGS –Program and attach Poppy Jasper to the dog's harness to help in aiding his/her training and assistance with humans.

THUNDERSTORM ISSUES –Make sure you have Eagle's Eye attached securely to the animal's collar/harness when thunderstorms approach to ease fear and anxiety levels.

THYROID PROBLEMS –Hold Rhodochrosite in your dominant hand and slowly turn this clockwise over the thyroid area for 15 minutes or as along as the animal will allow.

TICKS –Make a Black Coral gem elixir, charging for 30 minutes, and thoroughly mist the entire animal or area of concern. Repeat every 3 days when necessary.

TONGUE PROBLEMS (GENERAL) –Make an Aqua Aura and Clear Quartz gem elixir, charging for 1 hours, and place 5 drops in the animal's mouth or 10 drops in the water container.

TONGUE WORMS (REPTILES) –Make a Rutilated Quartz gem elixir, charging for 2 hours, and place 5 drops of this charged water in its water container. Next, place this crystal pointing towards the animal's general area of resting to help heal this issue on a consistent basis.

TONSILLITIS –Use an Aquamarine gem elixir, charging for 2 hours, and place 10 drops in the animal's mouth three times a day.

TOYS IN WATER DISH – Charge and program the water in the animal's water dish with a Clear Quartz crystal every day. After the water is replaced in the morning, attach the Clear Quartz to the underside of the water dish. Repeat every day until the energies balance out.

TRACKING –Program and attach Staurolite to the animal's collar/harness to increase his/her tracking scent.

TRAINING ISSUES (GENERAL) –Make sure you hold a programmed Red Jasper in your dominant hand when working with training issues for increased results. You can also attach a programmed Red Jasper to the animal's collar/harness for a stronger connection.

TRAVELING ISSUES –Make a Citrine gem elixir, charging for 1 hour, and give the animal 5 drops before travel time. You can also secure a piece of Citrine to the animal's crate, cage, harness, or collar during travel periods.

TRICHODINA (FISH) – Secure one Ruby and one Sapphire on opposite ends of the aquarium to balance this energy issue.

TRIMMING NAILS – Make sure to surround the animal with Obsidian during a nail trimming session. You can even hold one in your opposite hand while you are working on his/her nails.

TRUST ISSUES – Program and attach Angelite and Rose Quartz to the animal's collar/harness to have a more trusting relationship.

TUMORS – Hold a Black Phantom Quartz above the area of the tumor. Turn this counter-clockwise for 2 minutes, and then clockwise for 2 minutes. Slowly move the crystal up an away from the area such as a sweeping motion to deeply pull out stagnant energy build up. Repeat as necessary.

ULCERS – Place two Clear Quartz crystals on either side of the ulcer area, and hold an Agate above the area. Allow the animal to relax for 15 minutes and repeat as needed.

UNDESCENDED TESTICLES – Program and attach a Carnelian to the male's collar for this issue.

UPSET STOMACH – Place two Clear Quartz crystals on opposite sides of the animal, and hold a Topaz over the stomach area, turning clockwise to release any stagnant issues.

URINARY PROBLEMS (GENERAL) – Place Carnelian, Hematite, and Citrine in an alternating crystal circle around the animal and allow them to rest for as long as they desire.

URINE LICKING – Make a Tanzine Aura Quartz and Carnelian gem elixir, charging for 1 hour, and place 10 drops of this on the animal's tongue twice a day. Lightly mist all areas that he/she is licking too.

VACCINES – Hold a Clear Quartz over the area of the vaccine and turn clockwise for 3 minutes five times a day.

VEHICLE ACCIDENTS – Surround the animal with Yellow Jasper and hold Peridot over the animal's heart chakra to calm energetic shock issues.

VELVET (FISH) – Attach Amber and Clear Quartz to opposite sides of the aquarium to balance out this issue.

VOMITING – Place Citrine over the abdomen and Turquoise at the back of the neck to balance out these energies and help stop vomiting issues.

WANDERING LAMENESS (GROWING PAINS) – Attach Coral and Turquoise to the animal's collar/harness for best results.

WALKING – STIFFLY/DIFFICULTY – Attach Blue Lace Agate and Leopardskin Jasper to the animal's collar/harness to help with stiffness or difficulty walking.

WALNUTS - For walnut consumption, use a Rhodochrosite and Pink Topaz combination over the stomach area for a 20-minute session.

WARTS – Make a Marascite gem elixir, charging for 30 minutes, and generously mist the wart area three times a day.

WATER CLEANSING – Hold a Clear Quartz Terminated crystal in your dominant hand and slowly turn the crystal clockwise 3 times before drinking to remove toxins. Cleanse after each use.

WEAKNESS – Program and securely attach Turquoise and Tourmaline to the animal's collar/harness to help with weakness issues.

WEANING BABIES – Make sure to have the babies surrounded with Ruby and Strawberry Quartz during the weaning process to help ease the vibrational frequencies on their energetic fields.

WEEPING/CREEPING FIG PLANT –For weeping or creeping fig plant consumption, use Black Tourmaline and Aventurine over the stomach area for a 30-minute session.

WHINING/WHIMPERING (EXCESSIVE) – Program and attach Angelite and Agate to the animal's collar/harness to calm this excessive behavior.

WHINNYING PROBLEM – Attach a Tiger's Eye to the horse's reins to help with whinnying issues. Cleanse every 14 days.

WHIPWORMS –Place Topaz, Jasper and Black Obsidian in an alternating crystal circle surrounding the animal. Allow the animal to remain in the circle for as long as he/she desires. Repeat three times a day.

WHISKER ISSUES – Make a Sapphire and Clear Quartz gem elixir, charging or 2 hours, and lightly mist the whiskers to balance any issues.

WHITE LINE DISEASE (HORSES) – Make a Brown Carnelian and Jasper gem elixir, charging for 2 hours, and thoroughly mist all areas twice a day.

WHITE SPOT DISEASE (FISH/ICH) – Attach a Clear Quartz crystal to each side of the aquarium and one Topaz to the top of the aquarium lid. Cleanse every 7 days.

WILD ANIMALS – Working with wild animals can be tricky, but also very rewarding. For a general healing, place an Amethyst and Angelite circular crystal grid outside. Make sure you can keep an eye on the grid so that the wild animals do not eat the crystals. They may however try to pick one up and carry this to his/her home for constant energy.

WING INJURY – Program and secure an Emerald to the underside of the bird's cage for best results. Cleanse every 14 days.

WINGS CLIPPED – To help calm a bird after getting his/her wings clipped, program Celestite and attach this to the underside of the bird's cage for 48 hours.

WOBBLERS SYNDROME SURGERY – To help heal issues after surgery for Wobbler's Syndrome, attach Petrified Wood and Smoky Quartz to the animal's collar/harness. For a more direct connection, surround the animal with alternating crystals and allow the animal to remain in this crystal grid for as long as they desire.

YEAST DOUGH - For yeast dough consumption, use Serpentine over the stomach area for a 30-minute session.

YOWLING (CATS) – Cleanse, program and attach an Amethyst and Clear Quartz to the animal's collar/harness as close as you can to his/her throat chakra.

Endnotes

Crystal Healing has always been a passion of mine, and I have enjoyed working with these wonderful pieces of Mother Earth for what seems like my entire lifetime.

It has been my pleasure being able to share this information with everyone in a variety of formats. I knew and understood my guides when they said I was now put on a pathway to write spiritual and healing books, but never dreamed it would encompass such joy being able to help millions of people with my work.

Remember to make the connection between your mind, body, and spirit to help yourself first. Once you have fully connected with yourself and the Universe as one, you can start to help others on their own spiritual pathway through life. Humans, and animals alike, need to connect and stay connected! You can do this. We all can do this!

Namaste

About Practical Crystal Healing Books

Nicole Lanning started writing her practical crystal healing books before she even know what they were or why she was doing them. Being a natural born empath and psychic intuitive growing up, Nicole had a quest for knowledge even as a child and teenager. She started working with crystals during this time and fallen in love with their energies. Many ask what led to these books and how they have been designed. It was simple for Nicole, as they were already written for her with her years of experience in this field. She started learning and growing in her own spiritual development through her late teenage years taking notes and perfecting her work to be able to offer this information to clients. She performed her own trials of what worked and what didn't and how the majority of people and animals responded to the crystal healings. Once she had reached her point in life that her guides said it was time to write her books, they all started flowing out. She had done the work and research and it was now time to offer this to the world in a wonderful and convenient format for millions to share!

Experience Nicole Lanning's other crystal healing books at: http://www.practicalcrystalhealing.com

- ❖ Practical Crystal Healing: 555 Tips & Techniques
- ❖ Practical Crystal Healing: 555 Tips & Techniques For Pregnancy & Early Childhood – TO BE RELEASED
- ❖ Practical Crystal Healing: 555 Tips & Techniques For Teenagers – TO BE RELEASED
- ❖ Practical Crystal Healing: 555 Tips & Techniques – For Men & Women – TO BE RELEASED

About Healing Art Forms Institute

Nicole Lanning founded Healing Art Forms Institute in 2000 with a dream in her heart. She wanted to help people and she wanted to reach as many people as she could. Nicole, knowing that her town was not as open as some others, decided to jump into the internet world and start on her dream. With that, Healing Art Forms Institute was born. At first, it was offering Reiki attunements, basic healings, and intuitive readings and has grown leaps and bounds from there.

Today, Healing Art Forms Institute offers accredited programs, degree programs, physical healing, spiritual and energetic healings, customized healings, and a wide variety of over 800 attunements to choose from. Nicole also offers her private psychic intuitive readings through Healing Art Forms sister site. Reaching millions of people through online abilities was a dream that Nicole focused on to come true, and now she is touching millions of hearts and souls with her Practical Crystal Healing series books!

Visit us for online programs, healings, readings, and much more! http://www.healingartforms.com

About The Author

Nicole Lanning is a natural born empath, psychic intuitive, and healer that has focused her life on crystal, energy, holistic, and spiritual teachings. She is the founder of Healing Art Forms Institute and has dedicated her life to sharing her wisdom so that others may grow and learn.

Nicole always knew she was different from other children growing up as an early Indigo child and having a passion and love for her guides. She has transformed her life, being raised in a very strict religious God-fearing background, into a successful Spirit loving entrepreneur. Her spirit guides had set her on an energetically enlightened pathway through many different venues, such as being an Ordained Minister, Spiritual Life Coach, Reiki Master Teacher, and a Certified Energy Healer. Through her work now with psychic intuitive readings, holistic teaching, spiritual healing, and over 60 of her own channeled energy forms, Nicole has been honored with accreditations through the International Natural Healers Association and the World Metaphysical Association.

For more information about Nicole Lanning, Healing Art Forms Institute, or Practical Crystal Healing series books, please visit:

http://www.nicolelanning.com
http://www.healingartforms.com
http://www.practicalcrystalhealing.com